A Contrastive Study of Function in Intonation Systems

Hituzi Linguistics in English

No. 15	*Japanese Loanword Phonology*	Masahiko Mutsukawa
No. 16	*Derivational Linearization at the Syntax-Prosody Interface*	Kayono Shiobara
No. 17	*Polysemy and Compositionality*	Tatsuya Isono
No. 18	*fMRI Study of Japanese Phrasal Segmentation*	Hideki Oshima
No. 19	*Typological Studies on Languages in Thailand and Japan*	Tadao Miyamoto et al.
No. 20	*Repetition, Regularity, Redundancy*	Yasuyo Moriya
No. 21	*A Cognitive Pragmatic Analysis of Nominal Tautologies*	Naoko Yamamoto
No. 22	*A Contrastive Study of Responsibility for Understanding Utterances between Japanese and Korean*	Sumi Yoon
No. 23	*On Peripheries*	Anna Cardinaletti et al.
No. 24	*Metaphor of Emotions in English*	Ayako Omori
No. 25	*A Comparative Study of Compound Words*	Makiko Mukai
No. 26	*Grammatical Variation of Pronouns in Nineteenth-Century English Novels*	Masami Nakayama
No. 27	I mean *as a Marker of Intersubjective Adjustment*	Takashi Kobayashi
No. 28	*Lexical Pragmatics*	Akihiko Kawamura
No. 29	*An Affect-Oriented English Pronunciation Instructional Design for Japanese University Students*	Junko Chujo
No. 30	*The Diffusion of Western Loanwords in Contemporary Japanese*	Aimi Kuya
No. 31	*Tag Questions and Their Intersubjectivity*	Hiromi Nakatani
No. 32	*Biliteracy in Young Japanese Siblings*	Joy Taniguchi
No. 33	*The Pragmatics of Clausal Conjunction*	Miyuki Nagatsuji
No. 34	*A Cognitive Linguistic Approach to Japanese Agrammatism*	Hiroko Ihara
No. 35	*English Prepositions in Usage Contexts*	Fumino Horiuchi
No. 36	*Integrated Skills Development*	Takayuki Nakamori
No. 37	*Perception and Linguistic Form*	Kiyomi Tokuyama
No. 38	*The* No More A than B *Construction*	Atsushi Hirota
No. 39	*A Contrastive Study of Function in Intonation Systems*	Ken-ichi Kadooka

Hituzi Linguistics in English

39

KEN-ICHI KADOOKA

A Contrastive Study of Function in Intonation Systems

HITUZI
SYOBO

Copyright © Ken-ichi Kadooka 2024
First published 2024

Author: KEN-ICHI KADOOKA

All rights reserved. Except for the quotation
of short passages for the purposes of criticism
and review, no part of this publication may be
reproduced, stored in a retrieval system,
or transmitted in any form or by any means,
electronic, mechanical, photocopying, recording
or otherwise, without the written prior
permission of the publisher.

In case of photocopying, electronic copying, and
retrieval from the network for personal use,
permission will be given upon receipt of payment
and approval from the publisher. For details please
contact us through e-mail. Our e-mail address is
given below.

Hituzi Syobo Publishing

Yamato bldg. 2f, 2-1-2 Sengoku
    Bunkyo-ku Tokyo, Japan 112-0011
Telephone: +81-3-5319-4916
Facsimile: +81-3-5319-4917
e-mail: toiawase@hituzi.co.jp
https://www.hituzi.co.jp/
postal transfer: 00120-8-142852

ISBN978-4-8234-1257-8
Printed in Japan

Preface

This volume is the collection of the papers in the field of phonology, based on the framework of SFL or Systemic Functional Linguistics. I have been working in linguistics following the SFL methodology for more than 35 years. My main concern has focused on the meaning and function realized by the clause intonation systems of various languages. One of outstanding results gained within the SFL tradition seems to be that of the analyses of the English clause intonation systems as in Halliday (1967a, 1970) and Halliday and Greaves (2008). When I found that the English clause intonation systems have such wide connotations from the perspective of the interpersonal metafunction, I realized the necessity to pursue the investigation, especially with the typological viewpoint. That is to say, the whole languages in the world can be classified into tone languages and the others. Those non-tonal languages should have some accent systems in the lexical level. Most of the lexical accent systems are to be classified as stress-accented, while pitch-accented languages are minor, typified by Japanese. Further, Japanese is characteristic in that morae are the basic unit of length rather than syllables: three syllables and four morae in *ojisan* (uncle) vs. three syllables and five morae in *ojiisan* (grandfather), and similar with *obasan* (aunt) vs. *obaasan* (grandmother).

I assume that these phonological differences of the tone languages and the stress- and pitch-accent systems in the lexicon should have some relation in the clause intonation systems. In general, the rising intonation in the clause-final positions suggests the intention of interrogation, which is not the case with some tone languages, e.g. Mandarin Chinese, because clause intonation is restricted due to the lexical tone.

More highly 'developed' function of the clause intonation systems would be the pragmatic ones suggesting speaker's subtle nuances toward the hearer(s). Examples of request for information, politeness, irony, strong assertion of the speaker and so on are shown in the above listed references.

When the more languages are subject to be investigated with regard to the phonology in the lexicon and the function and meaning of the clause intonation systems, the more insightful results will be gained typologically.

謝辞

　本書は、龍谷大学国際社会文化研究所2020～2021年度研究助成、課題名「節音調の機能に関する英語と日本語対照研究」の成果として、出版助成を得て刊行されました（叢書第35巻）。

　また本書編集と刊行については、ひつじ書房の松本功社長および長野幹氏にお世話になりました。ここに記して謝意を表します。

Contents

Preface		V

CHAPTER 1
Introduction

1.1	Introduction	1
1.2	English Intonation System	5
1.3	English Tag Questions	8
1.4	Japanese Accent and Intonation	9
1.5	Japanese Particles	11
1.6	The SFL Framework	13

CHAPTER 2
Language Catalogue

2.1	Introduction	17
2.2	Tripartite in Function of Intonation Systems	18
2.3	SIS and PIS	22
2.4	Classification of Each Language	23
2.5	Discussion in Language Families	31
2.6	Conclusion	32

CHAPTER 3
On the Multi-Layer Structure of Metafunctions

3.1	Introduction	35
3.2	American Structurism vs. SFL	38
3.3	The Definition of Three Metafunctions	42
3.4	The Concentric Structure of Three Metafunctions in Intonation	47
3.5	New Images of Metafunction	50

| 3.6 | Text Analysis: An Example | 52 |
| 3.7 | Concluding Remarks | 56 |

CHAPTER 4

English Intonation System
as Interpersonal Embodiment

4.1	Introduction	57
4.2	English Intonation System	59
4.3	English Tag Questions	60
4.4	The SFL Framework	62
4.5	English Jokes	63
4.6	Gradual Lowering	70
4.7	Summary	73

CHAPTER 5

The Interpersonal-Nuance Carriers in Japanese

5.1	Introduction	75
5.2	Rank Scales in the Semiotic System	76
5.3	Intonation	77
5.4	Final Particles	80
5.5	Modal Auxiliaries	83
5.6	Semantics vs. Pragmatics: Conclusion	87

CHAPTER 6

An Acoustic Analysis of the Punch Line
Paratone in the *Kobanashi* Stories

6.1	Introduction	89
6.2	Japanese *Kobanashi*	90
6.2.1	*Kamo to Negi*	91
6.2.2	*Abura-ya no Neko*	94
6.2.3	*Kaita Mon ga Mono Iuta*	99
6.3	Conclusion	107

CONTENTS   IX

CHAPTER 7
Chinese Particles

7.1   Introduction   111
7.2   Chinese Particles   112

CHAPTER 8
CV Variations and Relative Productivity

8.1   Introduction   119
8.2   CV Variations   120
8.3   Relative Productivity   124
8.3.1   Korean   125
8.3.2   Japanese   127
8.3.3   Chinese   130
8.4   Conclusion   131

CHAPTER 9
Conclusion

                                                        133

References   137
Index   145

CHAPTER I

Introduction

1.1 Introduction

The most important purpose of this chapter is to testify that various systems to indicate personal-related subtle nuances can be uniformally explicable under the rubric of interpersonal metafunction within the framework of the Systemic Functional Linguistics[1] (henceforth abbreviated as *SFL*), though they are expressed in assorted ways from one language to another. This is to show that SFL is an appropriate model for grasping the interpersonal dimension even though it is expressed with diverse systems across languages, such as intonation in English, and particles in Japanese and Chinese.

The subject languages and the categories concerned with the interpersonal meaning are: English, whose intonational system is well documented so far; Japanese and Chinese in which particles play a major role in expressing both ideational and interpersonal meanings. It will be demonstrated in the following sections that these systems of intonation and particles function as the carrier of the nuances of interpersonal relationship.

Below are the first examples showing the differences in interpersonal meaning, one in English intonation system (1)[2] and another in Japanese particles (2):

(1) a. //1   you have / **beautiful** / eyes // (with a falling tone)
     b. //4   you have / beautiful / **eyes** // (with a fall-rise tone)
(2) a. kimi-wa   me-ga   kirei-da
        you-TOPIC   eye-NOM   beautiful   'your eyes are beautiful'
     b. kimi-wa me-wa kirei-da

The two utterances in (1) is a minimal pair with the difference of the intonation pattern and tonality (the detail will be presented in the next section), whereas in (2) is a pair of the alteration of the case-particle *ga/wa*[3]. Both in (1) and (2), the first instances (a), are unmarked in the interpersonal meaning, but the latter in

(b) are marked; both in English and in Japanese, a hidden message or an implicit suggestion is included that 'your eyes are beautiful but other parts are not so much ...'

Henceforth we will refer to this kind of the speaker's covert intention as *interpersonal nuances*. Tench (1996: 74) introduces the following interpretation with regard to the tone system in English, which also fits into the definition of the interpersonal nuances of the categories in other languages:

> ... the tone system produces contrasts in the communicative, or illocutionary, function; that is, they help to indicate differences between telling and asking, between commanding and requesting, between congratulating and wishing, and a whole host of similar functions that language is used to fulfil.

In a sense, interpersonal nuances reflect '[n]ot what they said, but the way they said it,' which 'refers to the mood of the speaker or the attitude shown to the addressee or the message' (*ibid.* : 20).

If we choose the option to make interpersonal nuance in (2)b less implicit, we can give an utterance below:

(2)   c. kimi-wa me-wa kirei-da kedo[4] ...
              though
        'though you have beautiful eyes, ...'

By the addition of an adversative conjunction particle 'kedo', the intention to explicitly refer to other parts than eyes is overt. This is in parallel with the English counterpart 'though you have beautiful eyes, ...' or 'your eyes are beautiful, but ...' It is needless to say that (2c) is not a complete statement by itself, but it will be one of the speaker's options not to finish the conclusion and leave it open. Though it is syntactically incanonical, it is stylistically possible because the concluding statement 'you are not beautiful except your eyes' will threaten the hearer's face; it is too rude to assume such attitude.

The third option to the unmarked statement (2a) is the attachment of a sentence-final particle (SFP) *ne*, as in below (2d):

(2)   d. kimi-wa me-wa kirei-da ne ...
                                  SFP

Compared with the conjuntioned version (2c) above, (2d) with the SFP *ne* is felt to be accomplished by itself. If the vowel of this particle *ne* is prolonged as *nee*, the whole statement will be more emotional; it would be felt as an exclamation.

Considering that the speaker's choices range far beyond the speculations in (2a–d) above in terms of age, gender and regional dialect, the stylistic variations will be uncountable, if we would stick to the ideational content of the utterance. In the SFL tradition, a series of the selections such as in (2a–d) are illustrated by the system network as follows:

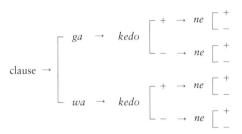

Figure 1.1: System network of *ga* and *wa*

These eight patterns presented here are only a tip of an iceberg among the plethoric variations of stylistic preferences.

In the spoken mode in each language, various phonetic and/or phonological parameters are combined to form characteristics of its own: stress accent vs. pitch accent, syllable timed vs. stress timed rhythm, syllable structure in terms of the combination of consonant(s) and vowel, patterns of consonant cluster, existence of consonant geminate, and so on. In this chapter, intonation systems are contrasted crosslinguistically adding the viewpoints of syntax, semantics and pragmatics.

Each intonation system of the individual languages presents assorted status of realization with regard to its function of expressing the meaning of the utterance. Such differentiation can be considered syntactically, semantically and pragmatically.

For the syntactic and semantic sphere, those utterances which can be distinguished only with the intonation alternation are subject to be studied. If the same succession of the phonemes are interpreted as a statement with the falling intonation and as a question with the rising counterpart, these utterances can be regarded as intonational minimal pairs. These intonational minimal pairs are observed and well documented in many languages, especially in such languages as English and German.

Pragmatic meaning refers to interpersonal connotations communicated by implicit manner of expression, such as irony, rhetoric question, roundabout entreaty. This is realized with intonation in English while it is final particles in Japanese[5].

4

The most important purpose of this chapter is to establish the legitimacy of the tripartite of pragmatic and syntactic intonation systems and tone languages in terms of the function of pitch movement. Such classification will be considered to be related to other phonological parameters in some implicational ways. These kinds of implications can be grouped into prototypical combinations of the parameters.

On the phoneme level, typological methodology has occupied a considerable position in phonology. This chapter will shed a new light into the phonological typology from the suprasegmental perspective of intonation, focusing on the level of function in which intonation works.

In what follows, I will exclusively use the term *prosody* referring to suprasegmental phonemes such as stress, accent, intonation, and tone. More comprehensive concept of prosody is, it seems, to consider these suprasegmentals in an interrelated manner; one of them is supposedly related to another. For example, intonation system is less predominant in tone languages with regard to syntactic/semantic/pragmatic function.

Let us consider in brief here how the parameters are organized by inspecting the well-documented languages.

English is a stress-timed language with plethoric patterns of consonant clusters, and the accentuation is mainly made with word stress. Intonation system is for conveying ideational and interpersonal meaning, in the level of clauses.

Swedish, another Germanic language, is similar to its cognate English in that stress play crucial role on the one hand while tone is also necessary in the lexical level. In the latter aspect, Swedish is comparable to Japanese[6].

It is well known that Japanese is syllable-timed, or mora-timed if we want to be more accurate. If the combination of a true consonant followed by a glide to be considered as a consonant cluster (C cluster), it has limited patterns of C clusters. Word accent with pitch contour is predominant while the intonation within clauses is functional to some extent, though lesser than in English.

Chinese is a tone language. Tone is assigned to each syllable/character, hence intonation within a clause is not so meaningful as in sentence-intonation oriented languages like English and German. As for Beijing Chinese, on the other hand, lexical stress is prerequisite phonologically though it is autonomously determined due to the distinction of tonic and atonic syllables. In Cantonese the situation is different; every syllable should carry its own tone and no counterparts for Beijing atonic tone.

In the chapters which will follow the present one, we will look into the combination of such parameters, probing various phonological parameters exemplified above. Further, some discussion will be made whether any systematicity can be found or not across the languages in terms of logical necessity of the composite of the parameters; for instance, which of the accent pattern of tone, pitch, or stress is most probable for those languages in which various types of consonant clusters are allowed.[7] This chapter will be the first step to investigate the correlation between the parameters.

The structure of this chapter is: sections 2 and 3 for English intonation and tag question, 4 and 5 for Japanese accent, intonation and particles, and 6 for the Chinese data. Preceding the concluding statements is section 7, some comments and suggestions on SFL.

1.2 English Intonation System

Intonation in English is one of the well documented subjects of the past studies among all of the phonological materials. It dates back as far as to the latter half of the eighteenth century (Cruttenden (1997: xv)). To name only a few among the recent publications, O'Connor and Arnold (1973), Bolinger (1978), Cruttenden (1997), and Gussenhoven (1986, 1992).

How many patterns of intonation contours to posit differs from one author to another. In either literature, meaning of the utterance and/or the situation, and the participants in the dialogue are taken into account more or less. The glosses assigned to each intonation pattern differ from one author to another. Chapter 6 of Tench (1996) concisely reviews the major literature of both of the patterns and the interpretations.

Since the 1960's, the SFL scheme has distinguished five simple and two compound tones (Halliday 1967a, 1970[8]):

(3) simple   1: fall   2: rise   3: level   4: fall—rise
      5: rise—fall
      compound 13: fall followed by level   53: rise—fall followed by level

Such detailed and minute distinction in the intonational system, of which semantic sphere will be reviewed soon in this section, is peculiar in English in that intonation is prerequisite in the spoken mode. Other languages do not necessarily utilize intonation in expressing and distinguishing interpersonal meaning.

Among the various phenomena in phonology, it is characteristic with the intonation system in English that intonation is deeply connected with the meaning and situation of the utterance, such as the speaker and the hearer and the relation between them. In this sense, it can be concluded that intonation in English is deeply concerned with the domain of semantics and pragmatics. Within the SFL framework, it would be concerned with interpersonal metafunction. The domain of SFL, and the traditional division of semantics and pragmatics will be a topic in section 7.

Tench (1996: 4) explicates the functions of intonation as 'what changes is its effect on the dialogue,' while 'the basic meaning ... has not changed' as for the utterance itself.

In the very beginning, Tench (1992: 161) defines clearly the SFL concepts of *tonality, tonicity* and *tone* (in the below citation, these terms are indicated with the capital letters):

> The three subsystems of intonation — TONALITY, TONICITY and TONE — are each involved in the speaker's organization of information. Whereas tonality represents the speaker's division of discourse into units of information, tone represents the speaker's classification of the STATUS of information. (emphasis original)

More comprehensive explanation for this triplet is in Tench (1996: 17-19). To supplement the definition of *tonicity* which is missing from the above excerpt, it is 'the structure of new and given information within each unit' (*ibid.*).

As shown with the system network in the Appendix of Halliday (1967a), which combines the English intonation system with the meaning of the utterances, it is understood that semantic and pragmatic consideration was indispensable within the SFL scheme of the lexicogrammar.

As is typically given with the examples below, the exactly same utterances can present diverse interpersonal nuances only with the alteration of intonation in English (Greaves: 1998):

(4)   To the question: *Do you like this painting?*
      //1 I like it // (neutral)
      //2 I like it // (challenging; *what makes you think I don't?*):
            defensive viewer when just accused of not appreciating the painting
      //3 I like it // (non-committal; *I don't object to it*): indecisive viewer
      //4 I like it // (reserved; *I do like it but...*): budget conscious buyer
      //5 I like it // (strong; *I really like it*): awestruck art critic

One of the possible problems in these *interpretations* is that too much situation is presupposed outside the linguistic facts. Additionally, it is certain that these intuitional data are not obtainable by non-native speakers. These situations and supposed speakers should be understood as typical realizations of the *artificial* examples above. More important is the fact that such subtle suggestion can be made only with the alteration of the intonation patterns.

The first instance of the same kind of set is found in Halliday (1970: 24), in which only intonation is altered:

CHAPTER I INTRODUCTION 7

(5) //1 ∧ he / could do //⁹ (simple statement)
　//2 ∧ he / could do // 　('is that what you think? could he?')
　//3 ∧ he / could do // 　('I think he could, but it's of no importance')
　//4 ∧ he / could do // 　('but he won't', 'but it won't help you', etc.)
　//5 ∧ he / could do // 　('so don't you imagine he couldn't!')

The postulated situation is less elaborated than in (4) above in that, for exam-ple, the speaker is not identified, but the basic concept lying the alteration of the typical intonation patterns is consistent since Halliday (1967a, 1970) or even before them: intonation is the only key which distinguishes the interpersonal nuances. In Tench's (1996: 21) wording, 'intonation has been solely responsi-ble for the expression of attitude.'

It is also the case with not only the complete set of five simple tones as in (4) and (5) but also with the two, three and four combinations that such subtle nu-ances are conveyed with the intonation pattern.

What about the Japanese equivalent to each Tone patterns 1 through 5 in (5)? Let us look at the following Japanese versions corresponding to each of (5):

(6)　a. kare-wa　dekiru (yo)
　　　he-TOP　can　　SFP
　　b. kare-wa　dekiru ka　　　na
　　　　　　　INTER　SFP
　　c. kare-wa dekiru darou　kedo …
　　　　　　　　　　would though
　　d. kare-wa dekiru darou kedo …
　　e. kare-wa dekiru yo

The difference between Tone 3 and 4 in (5) can not be explicitly declared in Japanese, so (6c) and (6d) are glossed undifferentiated. The parenthesized SFP *yo* in (a) is optional.

Contrary to English, Japanese intonation does not function to distinguish such minute interpersonal nuances denoted in (5). Instead, Japanese SFPs help suggest these subtle implications. The conjunctive particle *kedo* functions as a adversative conjunction on the one hand and an SFP on the other. It is desirable for the speaker to continue the utterance until it is perceived to be formally end-ed, but the style (6c, d) is also possible.

The modal auxiliary *darou* shows itself in (6c) and (6d), but not in (6a, b, e). If we interpret the original utterance in English as implying 'he could do if he wanted,' this modal *darou* would be necessary in the Japanese counterpart (6a) (*kare-wa dekiru darou*), but still not in (6b, e):

8

(6)′ b. * kare-wa dekiru-darou ka na
     e. * kare-wa dekiru-darou yo

Further consideration on modal auxiliary will be made in later chapters.

1.3 English Tag Questions

There is no exact counterpart in English to the particles in Japanese and Chinese. We can point out that the discourse particles (*DPs*; Schourup (1985) is the first attempt to highlight DPs from the linguistic perspective) such as *you know*, *I mean*. Tag questions in English are functionally and semantically similar to them to some extent. In this section we will examine the similarities and differences between the two systems of tag in English and SFPs in Japanese. The consideration of English DPs will be given to a next opportunity.

Tench (1996: 4) gives an explanation that the tag with the falling pitch 'sounds as if you are pretty sure of your facts': if it is with a rising pitch, 'you will sound as if you are not so sure of your facts.'

English tag clauses convey varied connotations *vis-à-vis* untagged counterparts. Typically they are demanding of consent and confirmation, and less generally information-seeking, which is almost analogous to mere interrogation without tags. The former will be realized with the falling pitch and the latter with the rising tone. Pragmatic background behind the demanding of consent and confirmation is that the speaker knows the answer or the circumstances beforehand.

Below is an instance of the English tag question (quoted from Quirk *et al.* (1985: 1600)), with the indication of a rising nucleus (shown with an acute accent) in the main clause followed by a falling nucleus (a grave accent) in the tag[10]:

(7) She was | looking HÁPpy tonight| | WÀSn't she|

For the untagged version (*she was looking happy tonight*), Quirk *et al.* (1985: 1600) comments as follows:

> This would make it not a question but a polite suggestion that a (confirmatory) comment would be welcome.

In the tagged one, this nuance 'might be expanded' (*op. cit.*, p. 1600).

In Japanese, instead of tag questions, such confirmatory process is expressed with the addition of sentence-final particles, as the following translation of (9) show:

(8) a. kanozyo-wa   siawase-sou   dat-ta
       she-TOP   happy-looking   ASSERT-Past
    'she was looking happy'

   b. kanozyo-wa siawase-sou dat-ta yo   ne
                                    SFP   SFP
      'she was looking happy, wasn't she?'

(a) is the plain version without an SFP, and (b) is the 'tagged' counterpart. The double particles 'yo ne' in (b) corresponds to a tag in English. In my observation, a prominence falls on this confirmation in Japanese — often the vowel of the SFP *ne* is prolonged as *nee* and with the falling nucleus on it. This is so that the intention to ascertain the statement should be emphasized.

1.4 Japanese Accent and Intonation

In this and the next section, we will look at how interpersonal nuances are embodied in Japanese. Before going to the argument in Japanese particles in the next section, let us briefly look at the Japanese intonation/accent system.

As far as I know, the Japanese intonation system has not been subject to integral analysis such as in English. This is because intonation does not function as carrier of interpersonal nuances in Japanese. Instead, sentence-final particles play major roles in the domain of semantics and pragmatics.

What is called *accent* in Japanese is the contour in pitch[11], unlike the stress placement system in English. While intonation system is to be contrasted in the level of the sentences in English, Japanese accent system is valid in distinguishing the minimal pairs in the stratum of words, as in below (my own accent — basically belongs to the Keihan dialect —, which is drastically different from the Tokyo accent):

(9) hasi   'chopstick'   hasi   'bridge'   hasi   'edge'
    L-H   H-L   H-H

In the sense that these make minimal pairs, it is certain that pitch accent can be regarded as phonemes in Japanese.

On the other hand, the Japanese language makes use of the intonation system in the stratum of sentences, though its usage is more restricted than in English. One of the few instances is the rising intonation in interrogative utterances.

Below is the minimal pair with the falling and rising tone in the utterance final positions:

(10) a. sou-desu   ka   (with a falling tone)   'Oh, I see.'
      so-COPULA   SFP
    b. sou-desu   ka   (with a rising tone)   'Is that so?'
                INTERROGATIVE

(a) is a response in which the speaker chimed in with what was said before, while (b) is a mere interrogation to the previous statement asking whether it is true or not. Here (b) requires the answer by the rising intonation, but (a) does not. It is a universal inclination that rising tone symbolizes the query for information (see, for instance, Halliday (1994: 302)).

Another minimal pair in intonation distinction:

(11) a. kore   taberu   no   (with the rising intonation)
      this   eat   INTER   'Do I eat this one?'[12]
    b. kore   taberu   no   (with the falling intonation)
                    IMPERATIVE   'Eat this one!'

As well as the pair in (9) above, the contrast shown here reflects the colloquial and informal situation of the utterance. Of the two, (b) is typically understood as in a situation that the mother is telling her young child to eat something. Such style is seldom adopted for addressing an adult.

In contrast with the English intonation system for which so many studies are accumulated, the intonation system in Japanese has been a rather minor subject from the semantic perspective. Vance (1987), an introductory reading on Japanese phonology, does not found an independent chapter nor section on sentence intonation. Nor is it argued in detail in Sugito, Kunihiro et al. (1997) , Jo-o (1998). Though some phonetic descriptions of the pitch contour pattern in the whole utterances are found in e.g. Saida (1997), Sugito (1997), those are rare in which semantic consideration is incorporated into them. Koori (1997) is one of the few exceptions to this tendency.

It is now evident, however, that the Japanese intonation system is parallel to that of English as an interpersonal nuance carrier, though its systematicity and the semantic range which it covers are limited.

1.5 Japanese Particles

At the beginning of this section, it must be noticed that it is not the purpose here to detect the entire system of the Japanese SFPs. It is enough at the moment to present the minimum examples of the Japanese SFPs participating in the interpersonal nuance distinctions.

The Japanese SFPs, though those listed below are only a few among them, denote the modal meanings such as interrogation, imperative, exclamation, consent and confirmation:
(12) ka, na, no, koto, zo, wa, yo, tomo, ne, sa
It is distinctive in Japanese SFPs that each item is far from homogeneous as regards to age, gender, and geographical origin of the speaker. Common with all of them are that they are colloquial and informal. The above entries are typical with the Tokyoite speakers; *zo, tomo* almost exclusively belong to the utterance by the male speakers, while *no, wa* are those of the female counterparts.

Among the various modal meaning denoted by the SFPs, some are concerned with the syntactic and semantic structure — interrogative, imperative, prohibition —, and others with interpersonal nuances of exclamation, demanding consent, confirmation, attention-calling, and hesitation. In a system network, this dichotomy can be illustrated as below:

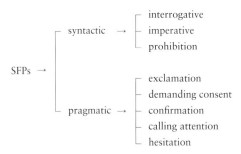

Figure 1.2: System network of SFPs

Of these categories, some such as the interrogative *ka* have been considered so far in relation to the clause intonation system. We will concentrate on the latter group in the rest of this section, as they would be parallel to English intonation and the Chinese particle systems.

The first category is the clauses of exclamation:

(12) a. kirei-da   naa
     beautiful   SFP   'How beautiful!'
   b. //1 ∧ it's / **very** / beautiful //

This type of the emotional announcement is akin to English clauses initiated with *How, What*. Another possible substitute in English is of a phonological nature as in (b): to emphasize with prominence falling on the modifier, in this case *very*. Semantically, such emphasis on the modifier is comparable to exclamatory clauses. The direct 'translation' of English *How beautiful!* into Japanese is *nante kirei (nan-darou)!*, which sounds too theatrical and showy, and is seldom to be uttered.

Next to be examined is demanding consent, and the resembling category of confirmation:

(13) a. atui   ne
     hot   SFP   'It's hot, isn't it?'
    b. kyou wa   kayoubi   dat-ta   ne
      today TOPIC Tuesday   COPULA-PAST SFP
      'It's Tuesday today, isn't it?'

As the English translations manifest themselves, these categories of the demanding of consent and confirmation in Japanese are perfectly in agreement with tag questions in English. The most curious point with these categories is that the SFPs are obligatory in them. When speaking to another person / other people, they are ungrammatical without SFPs:

(13)′a. *atui

    b. *kyou-wa kayoubi dat-ta

These versions (13)′ are acceptable if they are spoken to the speaker himself/herself. In this regard, the interpersonal aspect is mot important with these categories than in others — exclamation, attention-calling and hesitation — in which SFPs are optional.

The next examination is on the category of attention-calling:

(14) abunai   yo!
     dangerous SFP   'Danger! / Watch out!'

As a function of the clause, it needs no more explanation than the label *attention-calling*. The possible situations suitable to this utterance will be of great diversity: a car is approaching to the hearer, or something is in front of the hearer while he/she walking and looking away from it, and so on. When any of the SFPs are attached, the utterance became tedious, as if any serious danger were far away.

The last consideration is on hesitation, or the self-questioning:

(15) dou   si-you   ka   na
     how   do-FUTURE   SFP   SFP   'What shall I do?'

The English translation is with the intention of self-questioning, and it will be strengthened with the level intonation — tone 3. Opposite to the examples in (13) above and not in (13)′, this category is mainly construed as self-utterance; in other words, this class of utterances are not intended to talking to others as communicating something.

To conclude this section: the entire system of the Japanese SFPs would be enormous and need large amount of data and argumentation. As far as that which has been done in this section, however, it is clarified the category of Japanese SFPs embodies rich varieties of the interpersonal nuances. The English equivalents of the nuances implied in Japanese are: exclamatory clauses, phonological prominence, tag questions and intonation. These correspondences will be diagrammed in the following chapters.

Though there are numbers of similarities between Japanese and Chinese SFPs, the direct comparison has not been made in this section. That will be one of the topics to be contrasted in the following chapters.

1.6 The SFL Framework

One of the major advantages of SFL is, it seems, that any text can be subject to analysis whether it may be written or spoken. This entails naturally that suprasegmental phonemes such as pitch, stress, and intonation are parallel to syntactic categories such as nouns, adjectives and verbs in that they constitute semiotic code — language — as a whole. In this regard, SFL is quite different from the exclusively syntax-oriented approach to language, represented by that of Chomsky.

Under the SFL framework, languages are considered to be an interacted compound of semiotic code and the culture surrounding it. In those linguistic methodology other than the SFL approach, the similarity might have not been captured between intonation in English and the SFPs in Chinese and Japanese, with regard to the interpersonal nuances.

Under the rubric of *interpersonal metafunction*, those categories belonging to the spoken and the written modes can be contrasted directly. For the more detailed comparison, the framework should be strengthened.

In my understanding, there is one criterion to distinguish semantics from pragmatics; semantics is related in the ideational difference, whereas pragmatics is not. When just examining the instances in this chapter so far, we can see that the distinction between these two approaches is not always clear-cut. The distinction of the case particles *wa/ga* in Japanese, as briefly acknowledged in section 1, is of a syntactic nature in that topic and nominative case is marked respectively; it is pragmatically significant when we face the minimal pair such as (2a) and (2b). In the SFL scheme, such discernment itself is meaningless.

As a matter of fact, however, the SFL framework is constructed upon the English basis. Its typical example is Halliday (1994) in which intonation system is woven into the information structure Given + New. But now that it has been demonstrated so far in this chapter that the interpersonal nuances expressed in English intonation are realized with SFPs in Japanese and Chinese, the grammars of the two languages should be quite different from that of English as depicted in Halliday (1994). The contrast among these three languages will be diagrammed in the following chapters.

It seems unexpected that the intonation patterns bear various interpersonal nuances in English on the one hand, but it is excluded from the argumentation on the polarity and modality system in Chapter 4 in Halliday (1994). Contemplating that intonation is indispensable in the expressing of interpersonal nuances in the spoken mode, my suggestion is that it should be incorporated into the SFL system.

The strict definition of the *interpersonal nuances* should be elaborated within the Systemic scheme; and to what extent it is valid, the relative position to the ideational and textual metafunctions, and so on.

Notes

1 Halliday (1994) is the most introductory and fundamental reference of the Systemic linguistics.

2 The notations of the intonational system is after Halliday (1994): single slash for foot boundary, double slash for tone boundary, bold type for nuclei.

3 Hinds *et al.* (1987) is a volume of the collection of the papers on the case-particles *wa* and *ga*.

4 In (2c), the use of 'kedo' is informal and/or colloquial. More formal/literal forms will be 'keredo' or 'keredomo.'

5 Kadooka (1999b) discusses the interpersonal metafunction of sentence-final particles of Japanese and Chinese, together with the pragmatic function in the English intonation system. Katagiri (1997), on the other hand, is a paper combining the viewpoints of intonation phonology and sentence final particles.

6 For a brief summary of the intonation system of Swedish, see Gårding (1998) and the bibliography therein.

7 At present, the following correlation is in the author's idea; in those languages with rich system of C clusters, typically represented by English, tend to be stress timed and with pragmatic

CHAPTER I INTRODUCTION 15

intonation.

8 Halliday (1967a: 7) mentions that the basic concepts of the intonation system in English further dates back to early 1960s.

9 A caret (∧) signifies a silent beat (Halliday (1994: 294)).

10 The notations here are after the one in Quirk *et al.* (1985): thin verticals are symbols of boundaries of tone units; thick one is the terminal boundaries; nuclei are designated by capitals.

11 Pierrehumbert and Beckman (1986) and Kubozono (1995) are detailed argumentation on the Japanese accent system.

12 It is needless to point out here that the subject is not explicit in Japanese; so it is possible to interpret this utterance as indicating 'Do you eat this one?' But the latter is less probable since to ask someone if he/she wants to eat something may imply that the one who asks himself/herself wants to eat it, which may sound impudent.

CHAPTER 2

Language Catalogue

2.1 Introduction

Intonation can be defined as the move of pitch in the domain larger than one word. It is connected with semantics, and to syntax in the lesser extent, in that the identical utterance can make different connotation with the alteration of intonation pattern. As observed in many languages, a particular statement is interpreted as assertion when terminated with a falling tone, whereas it is decoded as an interrogation with a rising intonation.

It is inconsistent from one language to another to what extent intonation patterns are minutely dissected and phonologically systematized. A rough distinction between affirmation and interrogation such as above mentioned seems fairly universal; it is found in many of the non-tone languages. English is more noticeable in that elaborated system of intonation is used by the native speakers, and it has been well studied into the accumulation. To name only a few: O'Connor and Arnold (1973), Halliday (1967a, 1970), Bolinger (1978), Cruttenden (1997), Gussenhoven (1986, 1992) and Tench (1996). Since the references listed at the end of this volume is far from exhausting, readers should refer to that in Kadooka (1999b).

Hirst and Di Cristo (1998b) is an accumulation of the description on intonation systems of the twenty languages, with the intention of integrating the style of each chapter as unanimously as possible. The names of the languages and the authors are as follows:

(1)   American English (Dwight Bolinger), British English (Daniel Hirst),
      German (Dafydd Gibbon), Dutch (Johan't Hart),
      Swedish (Eva Gårding),   Danish (Nina Grønnum),
      Spanish (Santiago Alcoba, Julio Murillo),
      European Portuguese (Madalena Cruz-Ferreira),
      Brazilian Portuguese (João Antônio de Moraes),

French (Albert Di Cristo), Italian (Mario Rossi),
Romanian (Laurentią Dascălu-Jinga),
Russian (Natalia Svetozarova),
Bulgarian (Anastasia Misheva, Michel Nikov),
Greek (Antonis Botinis), Finnish (Antti Iivonen),
Hungarian (Ivan Fónagy), Western Arabic[1] (Thami Benkirane),
Japanese (Isamu Abe), Thai (Sudaporn Luksaneeyanawin),
Vietnamese (Đõ Thê Dung, Trán Thien Huong, Georges Boulkia),
Beijing Chinese (Paul Kratochvil)

The names of these languages are part of the titles of the chapters in Hirst and
Di Cristo (1998b); the title of Bolinger's chapter is, for instance, 'Intonation in
American English.' The same is true for the other languages. Instead of listing
in the bibliography at the end of this chapter, (1) will substitute the records of
the references consulted for these 20/22 languages.

If we count American/British English and European/Brazilian Portuguese
separately, the number of the languages attested is 22. Needless to point out,
these selections are not made in proportion with the number of the existing language families of the world. 17 out of 22 belong to the Indo-European family.
With this regard, this language catalogue is not idealistic from the typological
perspective in that the proportion of the existing natural languages is not reflected on the numbers of the languages investigated, which is pointed out by
the editors themselves (Hirst and Di Cristo 1998a:3). However, we will make
this a starting point and pursue whether we can find some meaningful implicational correlations between the parameters and the languages.

Of these 22 languages, three are tone languages belonging to the same phy-
lum of the Sino-Tibetan family: Thai, Vietnamese and Beijing Chinese. Then
the other 19 languages can be bifurcated into syntactic and pragmatic intonation systems.

In short, only pragmatic intonation systems carry interpersonal nuances defined in Kadooka (1999b). In syntactic intonation system languages, only the
basic semantic/syntactic differentiation is made: statement with falling pitch
contour and question with rising intonation for instance. The detail of these
points will appear in the following sections.

2.2 Tripartite in Function of Intonation Systems

In this section I would like to suggest the tripartite classes in the functional domain of intonation systems: pragmatic, syntactic and tone languages. This terminology seems inconsistent in that the category 'tone languages' is

CHAPTER 2 LANGUAGE CATALOGUE

heterogeneous to those of pragmatic and syntactic functions of intonation. Below are the explanations for each of the three categories.

The pragmatic classes are those in which interpersonal nuances, in the sense defined in Kadooka (1999b), are mainly realized by intonation patterns when one intends to imply the nuances implicitly. The typical case is English. The intonation system of this class is the most advantageous use among the tripartite classification. It was testified in Kadooka (1999b) that tag questions in English are functionally equivalent to final particles in Japanese and Chinese to some extent. But the interpersonal nuances carried by tag questions are much less eloquent than intonation in English.

Those which belong to the syntactic category are probably universal, from the statistical perspective in that the intonation makes the minimal pair of declarative and interrogative statement; falling intonation stands for the former and the rising the latter[2]. Such 'basic' distinction can also be observed in the pragmatic class. That is to say, there is an implicational order in the two categories in that if a given language utilizes pragmatic intonation function, syntactic distinction is prerequisite in that language, but not *vice versa*.

The third group, tone languages overlap with the accentual categories. It is meant that in tone languages contour movement is reserved for distinguishing lexical categories, hence sentence intonation is essentially insignificant. Syntactic function is subsidiary or almost deficient in these languages. One of the representative examples of this class is Chinese, which is supported by the following fact that the description in Kratochvil (1998) on Beijing Dialect of Modern Chinese, one of the collections in Hirst and Di Cristo (1998b), is devoted to that of tone system of that dialect, not mentioning on the intonation system in the clause level[3].

Definitionally, it can be posited that tone languages are paraphrased as those which distinguish the pitch contour inherent to all the lexical categories. In other words, Japanese is not a tone language in that some of the lexicon are recognized by the pitch accent but not all, as exemplified below:

(2) tonal patterns on the noun *hasi* (my own accent[4]):
hasi 'chopstick'   hasi 'bridge'   hasi 'edge'
L-H   H-L   H-H

Notice, however, that H/L pitch contour is not inherent in all the lexical categories in Japanese. Typical are functional word such as case particles *wa, ga*:

(3) a. hasi   ga   ore-ta
L-H   H   L-H-L
chopstick NOM   broken

b. hasi ga ore-ta
   H-L L L-H-L
   bridge
c. hasi ga   ore-ta
   H-H   H   L-H-L
   edge NOM broken

Here the pitch height of the particle *ga* is dependent on that of the precedent mora; it is realized as low in (b) while it is high in (a, c). This is an evidence that Japanese is not a tone language, in which all the lexical items should be assigned its inherent tone.

Some of the spontaneous utterances in Japanese entail characteristic intonation patterns; unmarked prominence indicated with underlines in the following instances based on my own observation:

(4) a. so+-desu ka   (falling intonation):   'I see.'
     b. so+-desu ka[5]   (rising intonation):   'Is that so?'
     c. so+-desu ka+   (falling-rising):   'I don't think so.'
     d. so++-desu ka   (rising-falling):   'Oooooh, I see.'

The difference between (a) and (b) is basically a syntactic one in that confirmation (a) and questioning (b) of the hearer are distinguished with the intonation.

The intonation pattern in (c) and (d), on the other hand, are pragmatic. (c), with the fall-rise nucleus in the particle *ka*, entails the prolongation in the vowel of that syllable, suggesting the strong doubt of the hearer against the speaker's statement. (d) with the rise-fall pattern[6] on the first syllable sounds theater-like effect; if such intonation is heard in the daily conversation, the intention of the speaker may interpreted with some purpose: the hearer is greatly surprised to know the fact for the first time, or he/she should like to pretend so.

Notice that the utterances with the pragmatic intonation patterns such as (4c, d) are absolutely rare in Japanese spontaneous speech. It will be difficult to find more examples like these. In this regard Japanese should be classified with the syntactic/semantic intonation system.

The criterion to divide pragmatic and syntactic/semantic systems is whether intonation mainly carries the interpersonal nuances or not; those intonation systems which plays crucial roles in communicating interpersonal nuances are pragmatic, while other means take place of such task in the syntactic/semantic system languages.

From the viewpoint of the function of intonation, (4a)-(4d) and (4b)-(4d) are alike respectively. The former pair displays hearer's confirmation of the speaker's statement, while the latter presents doubt about it.

CHAPTER 2 LANGUAGE CATALOGUE 21

The categorical difference in these two pairs derives from the alteration of syntactic/semantic and pragmatic functions. (4)a and b, those with syntactic/semantic function but not pragmatic, merely carry the intention of hearer's agreement and questioning, respectively. In (4)c,d, in addition to these 'basic' significations, 'distinguished' or pragmatic nuances are adjoined. (d) is in contrast with (a) in that exaggerated surprise is expressed with the rise-fall intonation in the first syllable. This exaggeration is for the hearer to win the speaker's favor. The theater-like effect is synthesized by the exceptional contour pattern of rise-fall and the extra-long vowel in *so++*. The speaker would realize after this hearer's response that the hearer is impressed by what the speaker had said. In (4c), hearer's doubt is multiplied with the fall-rise intonation, suggesting strongly that the hearer does not believe in what the speaker said at all. The speaker would feel embarassed by this hearer's emotional expression. These speaker's feelings are caused by the pragmatic function carried by intonation.

My hypothesis is that the interpersonal nuances suggested by pragmatic intonation in some languages are substituted by other means in other languages. It was shown in Kadooka (1999b) that final particles play major pragmatic role in Japanese and Chinese. If we postulate that in each language implicit communicative devices are prerequisite, in what way it is realized is different from one language to another. It is hardly imaginable, to put in other words, that interpersonal relationships between individuals would not go without subtle and/or minute conflicts in any culture, language should behave eloquently in the communication of interpersonal nuances.

As a framework for this tripartite, Campbell (1997:55-57) may be appropriate. His suggestion is that the levels of the correlation between semantic stratum and prosody can be classified into eight stages, including the phoneme-level distinction such as *oji-san* and *ojii-san* tagged as Seg/Pro. Lo[7]. According to his definition, intonation is a Pro. L4 distinction, labeling its function as *attitude* while its realization is tagged as *speech act*. Interpersonal nuances, the subject of Kadooka (1999b), seems to include his classification of L5: emotion — interpersonal and L6: sincerity — commitment[8]. It seems that the level L7: individuality — voice quality also belongs to the domain of pragmatics, but it is out of the scope of phonology. His main point is manifested in the title in Campbell (1997): "pragmatic intonation." This seems to be line with the aim of this chapter.

2.3 SIS and PIS

In Kadooka (2000), the function of the intonation systems was categorized into syntactic, semantic and pragmatic branches. Those which convey interpersonal nuances more dynamically and predominantly than the other means in a given language will be dubbed Pragmatic Intonation System (PIS). If, on the other hand, only the syntactic meanings are carried, or the pragmatic meaning is conveyed only partially and/or passively, they will be defined as Syntactic Intonation Systems (SISs), as exemplified with a back channel response *soo-desu-ka* in Japanese in Kadooka (2000: 41).

This tripartite of tone languages, SIS and PIS is in line with the phonological functions working in the levels of lexicon, sentence and discourse, respectively. In tone languages, pitch differentiation is realized in the lexical level, hence sentence intonation is invalid syntactically/semantically. In the languages of syntactic intonation systems, sentence intonation is useful as a resource to function syntactically/semantically. If the lexicon distinguishes each item with the pitch system, as in the case with Japanese, the situation resembles those in tone languages in that the pitch is lexically distinctive. But the difference is that such lexical distinction is not always necessary in SIS. Take Japanese for example, again. Pitch is the most distinctive with nouns, and less with verbs. In adjectives it is still less typical. The situation is in contrast with Beijing Chinese, a typical tone language in which all the lexical items should be realized with their inherent tone except certain limited categories such as final particles.

Pragmatic intonation is highly expressive to carry interpersonal nuances between the parties joining discourse. The borders between SIS and PIS may be difficult to draw in certain cases. In order to be classified as PIS, connotations conveyed by intonation must be demonstrative enough.

There would be two ways to divide the three categories of the languages of SIS, PIS and tone languages at the moment. The first one is to distinguish according to the existence/absence of the sentence intonation system. With this criterion, tone languages should be separated from the other two. The second one is to bisect by the interpersonal function of intonation; both tone languages and SIS languages belong to the same group in which the pragmatic expressiveness of intonation is subsidiary, while it is major in the PIS languages. To illustrate these two ways of division in the table below, dotted lines indicate that the two categories divided by them can be regarded as belonging to the same group:

From the comparison in this table, it is clear that the grouping does not necessarily remain exact when the criterion is altered. This is because the in-between category SIS is combined with tone languages in some cases and with PIS in the other. As for the pragmatic function of intonation for example, the absence in

Table 2.1: Tone languages, SIS and PIS

category	sentence intonation	pragmatic function
tone languages	none	none
SIS	yes	subsidiary / passive
PIS	yes	predominant / active

tone languages and the subsidiary role in SIS are regarded alike to each other, compared to the predominant role in PIS.

Now let us turn our eyes to the discussion on each intonation system.

2.4 Classification of Each Language

In this section, judgement will be made whether each intonation system listed in the catalogue in section 2 belongs to a SIS or a PIS, leaving aside the tone languages (Beijing Chinese, Thai, Vietnamese) since their status is evident from the definition. Below is shown the classification after the name of the language, except English and Japanese which have been verified in some depth in chapter 1. Examples will be adopted as many as possible, to demonstrate the classification.[9]

German: PIS

Gibbon (1998: 87), basing on the a precedent study[10], verifies that the intonation patterns of German are similar to those of British English[11], consisting of five simplex ones: falling (1), rising (2), level (3), falling-rising (4), and rising-falling (5). These patterns of intonation express the following meaning, parenthesized numerals corresponding the above patterns; here each systemic function such as *statements, questions, exclamations*, is classified into the two categories syntactic and pragmatic by the present author:

(5) syntactic : statements (1), questions (2)
    pragmatic: exclamations (1), non-final (2), progredience (3), incompleteness (3)
                uncertainty (4), certainty (5), obviousness (5)

It is understandable that the patterns one through five and meaning denoted by them are almost exact as those of the English intonation system. This is because Pheby (1975) adopts the Hallidayan scheme of the Systemic approach. It may be benefitable on the one hand in the sense that the two intonation systems are in parallel, hence the direct comparison is possible between them. If, on the

24

other hand, the German intonation system is exact as that of English, we must investigate whether the complex patterns of 13 and 53 in English are found in German or not. Table 2 in Gibbon (*ibid*: 89) presents more subtle subclasses of Mood, Tone and Function.

Dutch: PIS

In 't Hart (1998: 107), the function of the hat pattern[12], beginning low followed by rising and then ending in low, looking like a shape of a silk hat, is explicated as follows:

(6) ... although the hat pattern is the most adequate pattern to be used in neutral declaratives and interrogatives, it has been observed in many situations of which it was clear that peevishness, irony, preponderance, restrained anger or consolation was at stake.

From this short citation, the status of the Dutch intonation system is evident; it is a PIS, like its brother languages of German, Swedish and English. The varieties of connotation carried by intonation in Dutch are typical as speaker's secret intention.

Swedish: PIS

Though Swedish is similar to Japanese in that the lexicon is distinctive with pitch accent system, its intonation should be classified as a PIS, if we accept the explanation below (Gårding 1998: 121):

(7) ... there are contributions also from lexicon and syntax [in speech acts conveying the speaker's attitude, emotion and selected center of message: KK]. However, the modal and expressive signals of intonation are so strong that they may override other cues.

Considering that the Swedish intonation system has common function with the Japanese counterpart in the lexical level on the one hand, and share the pragmatic intonation function with English on the other hand, it should be posited that tone system in the lexical level and function in intonation — the distinction in SIS and PIS — are independent to each other.

Danish: uncertain

It is not explicit whether Danish intonation is a SIS or a PIS, while Grønnum (1998: 132) subdivides the phonological levels in Danish into the following six levels: text — sentence/utterance — prosodic phrase — prosodic stress group (foot) — stød — segments. Among these six levels, intonation should be related

CHAPTER 2 LANGUAGE CATALOGUE 25

to those of text and sentence/utterance.

Haberland (1994: 323), on the other hand, explicates as follows with regard to Danish intonation function:

(8) ... as far as clause types in Danish are marked by pitch contour, they are marked globally, in the entire clause, and not (*like in other Germanic languages like English and German*) by a typical contour in the last part of the clause only. This means that Danish has no sentence accent; in neutral sentences without contrast or focus accent, there is no particular stress group that is more prominent than others. *In this Danish is different from a closely related language like Swedish.* (Italics added)

Taking this statement — especially those italicized comments — into account, it seems better to classify Danish as SIS. As a conclusion, however, Danish will be excluded from the discussion in the next section, considering that there is no examples in Haberland (1994).

Spanish: SIS

It seems that the Germanic languages depend on intonation for communicating interpersonal nuances on the whole. Now let us turn our eyes to Romance languages. The phonological systems in Romance languages such as syllable structure, rhythm, accent differ from those of the Germanic languages. Alcoba and Murillo (1998: 159) give example of three patterns of 'Si' (yes) in Spanish:

(9) a. SI, SI (two tone groups, each falling)   'Yes, OK.'
     b. SI SI   (one tone group, falling)   'No, only a fool would believe that.'
     c. ¿SI?   (one tone group, rising)   'Is that so?'

Strictly speaking, these are not minimal pairs with intonation, but together with the modification in the repetition and number of tone group(s). Notice that these utterances are back channel responses, sharing commonality with 'soo/soo-desu-ka' in Japanese. This has led to the result that Spanish is classified as an SIS. To be judged as a PIS, intonational function should be more dynamic and active.

European Portuguese: PIS

In European Portuguese, various connotation can be conveyed with intonation, according to Cruz-Ferreira (1998: 171-173)[13]:

(10) a. está a choVER outra VEZ   (a high-falling tone)
        'it is raining again (and I cannot stand it)'

b. porque É que não DIzes o que PENsas? (a high-falling tone)
'why don't you speak your mind? (you are an idiot if you don't)'
c. SAI daQUI!! (a high-falling tone)
'get out of here!! (I won't tell you again)'
d. onde É que puSESte o meu caSAco?! (a high-falling tone)
'where have you put my coat? (I'm sick and tired of you misplacing it!)'
e. eu viVI na CHIna dez Anos (a rise-fall)
'I lived in China for ten years (but I never learned the language)'
f. tu SAbes quem É aquele TIpo? (a rise-fall)
'do you know who that chap is? (he's the one who was jailed for bigamy)'

Those interpersonal glosses parenthesized in each utterance verify the expressiveness of intonemes in European Portuguese, leading to a postulation that it is a PIS language.

Brazilian Portuguese: PIS

Though only with one type of utterance, the state of function of intonation in Brazilian Portuguese is judged as PIS. For the statement 'Fecha a porta' (close the door), the three patterns of command, request and suggestion are provided with the intonation contour (Moraes (1998: 187–188), in the subsection titled *Illocutionary acts and intonation*). These three concepts cannot be integrated into one category though they have some commonality of asking illocutionary acts, and distinguished only with intonation. In this regard, the intonation system of Brazilian Portuguese should be considered to function pragmatically.

In the discussion in the next section, European and Brazilian Portuguese will be treated as one language, since both variants are classified as PIS.

French: PIS

In describing the expressiveness of the French intonation system, Di Cristo (1998[14]: 208) states as follows:

(11) It is a well known fact that both intonation and non-verbal gestures are used to convey attitudinal meanings.

As the exemplification of an "implicative" (Di Cristo (1998: 208)) utterance *La téLÉ est caSSÉE* (the TV set is broken), a large rise-fall movement on the last syllable and the deaccentuation of preceding stressed syllable are illustrated by an F_o curve. Such pitch pattern as this one 'convey different meanings depending on the syntactic structure with which it is associated.' The detail is as follows (*ibid*, 208):

(12) For example, with the syntactic structure of a partial question, it means some kind of exasperation; with that of an imperative, a polite invitation, and so on.

As Di Cristo (1998: 208) concludes himself, however, 'a comprehensive description of expressive patterns needs more sophisticated frame of analysis.'

Italian: SIS
Table 1 in Rossi (1998: 223) suggests the commonality of stress and intonation morpheme between Italian and French, in which PA for pragmatic accent seems to be most related to the present pursuit. An explanation for this concept is given as 'which ... focalises an element of an utterance.' The examples shown there are those of focalization (a), postponed theme (b), marked theme (c) and so on:

(13) a. il nostro discorso, si avvia alla conclusione.
    'our speech is coming to its conclusion'
b. È molto femminile, mia faglia.   'she is very feminine, my daughter'
c. La maggioranza relativa ... non ve la vuol togliere nessuno
    'The relative majority? No-one will take it away from you'
d. Il potere, Lei può farlo sentire con delle decisioni.
    'power, you can make it felt with decision'

Considering that these statements are marked — focalization, postponed and marked theme —, it should be appropriate to regard that the Italian intonation system is subsidiary to the syntactic means as far as looking at these examples.

Romanian: SIS
Not enough in number, nor poorly in the quality of the examples in the sense that intonation is auxiliary as the responses to precedent questions, it would be proper to classify Romanian an SIS language. Below are some of the examples from Dascălu-Jinga (1998: 252-256)[15]:

(14) a. MAma   VIne   REpede.
          Top   Downstep
   (Mother is coming quickly)
b. MAma   VIne   REpede.
         Dwnstp   Top
   (Mother is coming quickly)
c. Dacă teCHEmă   cînd   ai să aJUNGI   aCOlo,   SPUne-mi.
   [Bottom   Btm Top][   ]
   (If he calls you when you get there, let me know)

d. Dacă teCHEmă cînd ai să aJUNGI aCOloSPUne-mi.
[   ][·   Btm   Btm   ·Top][   ]
(If he calls you, when you get there let me know)
e. SK facem fiecare cîte o încercare?   (Shall we all try?)
f. DE ce NU!   [Higher, Same, Lower]   (Why not!)
g. N-ai vrea sK mergi cu mine la film?   (You won't go to the cinema with me?)
h. DE ce NU!   [Same, Top, Bottom]   (Why "won't"?)

The pair (14)a, b is essentially a matter of emphasis, rather than a subject of intonation exclusively. The alternation of Top fallen on *REpede* in (a) and *VIne* in (b) is a consequence of the change of emphasis.

The only occurrence of a possible instance for proving the validity of pragmatic aspect of the Romanian intonation system is this (Dascălu-Jinga 1998: 252):

(15) a. Cînd VIne?   (When is he coming?)
     [Same Top, Bottom]
   b. Cînd   VIne?
     [Top, Lower   Higher, Bottom]

(15)a shows that the speaker wants to emphasize *VIne* for the purpose of contrast rather than the fully deaccented question word *cînd*. In (b), on the other hand, the speaker is more insistent, or even irritated for not being understood, the question *cînd* has two intonation peaks Top and Lower.

As a conclusion, intonation in Romanian *per se* is not eloquent enough to be a PIS. The feeling carried by double peak intonation in (16b) above is of primitive nature pragmatically, not suitable for the definition of PIS in the present study.

Russian: PIS

As Svetozarova (1998: 268) defines, the Russian intonation system is expressive in the following way:

(16) Emotional connotation such as surprise, doubt, distrust, and irony are usually expressed in Russian by means of various modifications of the question intonation: differences in the length of the stressed syllable, the sharpness and height of the rise, different phonation types (...).

With this explication, it would be suitable to classify Russian as a PIS. One of the instances to show this is as follows (Svetozarova (1998: 270)):

(17) a. иВАН чиТАет
    /i'van tʃi'tait/   (John is reading)
    [Top Top Bottom]
  b. иВАН чиТАет (It's John who is reading)
    /i'van tʃi'tait/
    [Top Btm   ]

In this pair in Russian, intonation patterns are altered together with the emphasis on 'иВАН' (John). In (a), the second syllable in 'иВАН' is raised in pitch, while in (b) the first syllable raised then fallen on the second. This alternation corresponds to a cleft sentence in the English counterpart.

Bulgarian: PIS

To summarize the function of the Bulgarian intonation system (Misheva and Nikov (1998)), it is the position of F_o peak that influences the attitudinal aspect of utterances most relatedly. They insist that the progressive force of the F_o peak is applied in typical WH-questions while it is the regressive force in declarative counterparts. Below is their account (*ibid*, 281):

(18) The intonation of emotionally loaded questions, the function of which is not to ask for information but to deliver information about the speaker's emotions (...), follows the basic regularities determined for statements: ...

An instance is given (*kak voima* (What's the matter?)) with falling and low rise tones, of which the latter sounds politer (*ibid*, 280). Considering that politeness is an important aspect of interpersonal relationship, intonation in Bulgarian has pragmatic sphere.

Greek: PIS

Botinis (1998) devotes one sub-section (2.4 Phrasing and discourse intonation) to the description of the function of the Greek intonation system as the means to suggest changes of sub-turn-units (STUs). A rise of pitch, for example, 'marks the intention of the speaker to keep his turn, ...' (*ibid*, 308). This kind of function to imply the turn of the speaker is crucial in discourse.[16]

Finnish: SIS

Though Iivonen(1998: 320) comments as follows, it is doubtful to consider Finnish as a member of PIS group:

(19) It is hardly true that the variation range of Finnish intonation is narrow in all circumstances.

By F_o delay, which seems to be akin to a pragmatic function of intonation, a meaning of hinting is suggested:

(20) a. Sy dänvika se on.   (F_o peak on *Sy*: A heart disease it is.)
     b. Sy dänvika se on.   (F_o peak on *dän*: A heart disease it is, sure)

This pair of F_o shift brings a type of contrast. Notice that this minimal pair is the gap of F_o peak, not a difference in the intonation patterns.

In conclusion, Finnish should be regarded as SIS as far as the data in Iivonen (1998) are concerned.

Hungarian: SIS

Fónagy (1998: 330) lists the below five patterns as the inventory of Hungarian prosodemes, utilizing the citation from some precedent studies[17]:

(21) 1. falling   2. rising-falling 3. falling-rising 4. rising 5. descending

Though morphologically distinctive as well as intonational, the examples are given in the main text (*ibid*: 333):

(22) a. Tett?   (he did): rising
     b. Tette?   (did he do it?): rise-falling
     c. Tetette?   (did he pretend to do it?): rise-falling

At a glance, these patterns look opposite to the universal ones that declaratives are realized with a falling tone and interrogatives with final rise. Though the patterns of rise and fall are inconsistent with the universal counterparts, it is certain that intonation is related to the discernment of declarative and interrogative.

With the increase of the number of syllables, the meaning is changed from simple to complex: declarative (a) — interrogative (b) — complex interrogative (c). For the addition of such meaning, intonation is subsidiary, however; suffixes are more predominant in the contrast of meaning. In this sense, it is determined that Hungarian is a SIS language.

Western Arabic: SIS

Investigating the examples in Benkirane (1998), no evidence is found to conclude that pragmatic function is included in the Western Arabic intonation system spoken in Morocco. Instead, declarative (23a) and interrogative (23b) are discerned as follows (Benkirane (*ibid*: 352–355):

CHAPTER 2 LANGUAGE CATALOGUE   31

(23) a. /ʒæ'bulha 'lma/   (They brought him some water)
        [Top   Btm]
     b. /ʒæbu lma'gæna/   (Did they bring the watch/meter?)
        [Top Btm]

As Benkirane (*ibid*: 354) states, 'the pattern for Yes/No questions is very similar
to that observed for statements: in both cases a rising-falling pattern is observed.' Though it seems insufficient with the data in Benkirane (*ibid*), the most
basic distinction of declaratives and interrogatives are confusing since both intonation patterns are alike to each other. Among the languages detested in
Hirst and Di Dristo (eds., 1998a), the Western Arabic intonation system is the
least helpful in expressing syntactic/semantic meaning.

2.5 Discussion in Language Families

To summarize the argument up to the previous section, the classification of
each intonation system with the criterion of the tripartite is as follows, exclud-
ing Danish and including English and Japanese; the languages are grouped into
the families/branches parenthesized in square brackets:

(24) PIS—9 languages
        [Germanic]:   English[18], German, Dutch, Swedish,
        [Romance]:   European and Brazilian Portuguese, French
        [Slavic]:   Russian, Bulgarian
        [other IE]:   Greek
     SIS—7 languages
        [Romance]:   Spanish, Italian, Romanian
        [Uralic]:   Finnish, Hungarian
        [Semitic]:   Western Arabic
        [Altaic]:   Japanese[19]
     tone languages—3 : Thai, Vietnamese, Beijing Chinese

The Indo-European family is further subdivided into the Germanic, Romance
and Slavic branches, since the label *Indo-European* is too big to grip all of them
at one time on the one hand, and so many languages are listed in proportion to
the others belonging to different families. Non-Indo-European languages are:
Uralic family of Hungarian, Finnish; Semitic Western Arabic; Altaic Japanese;
and Sino-Tibetan family of Thai, Vietnamese, Beijing Chinese. The following
characteristics can be pointed out with this result.

(25) 1. All the Germanic languages belong to PIS.[20]
    2. The Romance languages are divided into PIS (two languages) and SIS (three).
    3. All the Slavic languages belong to PIS, with only two instances.
    4. All the Uralic languages belong to SIS, with only two instances.

In general, each branch or family — especially Germanic, Slavic, Uralic — shows a tendency as a group in which intonation system behave similarly with regard to the pragmatic function, as far as these 19 languages in the catalogue are concerned.

When we enlarge the target to more diversified and numerous examples, the consequence is highly interesting from the typological viewpoint; non-Indo-European data must be reinforced in order to reflect the proportion of the existing languages of the world. If the result is akin to the one in this chapter, it is fruitful as a pilot study.

It would also be misleading to deduce some conclusion from the statistics in (25), still there would be some tendencies, however; the PIS languages are slightly more predominant in number than the SIS counterparts in nine to seven. Whether the gap is greater or smaller than this figure will depend on the selection of the targeted languages. Tone languages occupy the position of relative minority. With larger databases, the proportion occupied by tone languages will be known easily. Then, it will be necessary to divide the rest of the languages into SIS and PIS, with procedures done so far in this discussion.

2.6 Conclusion

In this last section of the present investigation, some problems to be solved in future will be briefly addressed as concluding remarks.

The first and the biggest one is the complementary distribution of the interpersonal nuances carried by intonation system and other means. It will be clearcut to take an example with one of tone languages. As neither syntactic nor pragmatic meaning is carried by intonation in them, other means are necessary to express syntactic function such as interrogative or pragmatic nuances. One of such realizations is the final particles in Chinese. In the PIS languages, various intonation patterns are predominant in carrying minute nuances, hence the role played by other means is relatively small. Kadooka (1999b) contrasts the three languages English, Chinese and Japanese in terms of how interpersonal nuances are realized linguistically.

It would need more minute examination which kind of connotation is expressed with syntactic and pragmatic function of intonation, respectively. To put differently, the definitions of the syntactic and pragmatic function should

CHAPTER 2 LANGUAGE CATALOGUE   33

be pursued more extensively. To point out concretely, F_o delay in Finnish is in a sense common to contrastive emphasis by sentence-stress in many of the languages worldwide, to be classified as one of syntactic functions; hint of sub-turn-unit change in Greek, on the other hand, is a type of pragmatic usage of intonation. Both are deviant from the typical realization of the two categories respectively, in that the syntactic function clarifies most universally the border between declaratives and interrogatives, and that the pragmatic one carries the speaker's interpersonal attitude.

Another question left unanswered here is whether there are any instances of non-tone languages or not whose intonation system are invalid in syntactic function of discerning declarative and interrogative. In other words, intonation system is not distinctive syntactically/semantically in such language, if any.[21]

A chance to argue the syntactic and/or pragmatic function in tone languages will be given in the next occasion. Some insist that syntactic and/or pragmatic function of intonation can be found in tone languages: e.g. Luksaneeyanawin (1998) for Thai.

Notes

1 Dialect spoken in Morocco.

2 Hirst and Di Cristo (1998a:39) state as follows in regard to this distinction:

Qualitative pitch differences relative to the distinction between statements and yes/no question are observed in dialects of Danish, Portuguese, Spanish, Romanian, Greek and Arabic. In addition to these six languages, Japanese seems to belong to the same category in that the plain statement and yes/no question can be minimal pair with the difference of intonation.

3 The editors themselves make the same kind of excuse as foreword to Kratochvil (1998).

4 My accent basically belongs to the Keihan dialect, which is drastically different from the Tokyo accent.

5 The assignment of the prominence to the last syllable *ka* is tentative. It may be that the first syllable *so+* be given as the same degree of prominence as that of *ka*. In order to *ka* to carry the rising nucleus, it should be more prominent than the other syllables in the utterance. If too much emphasis be laid on the last syllable, the message itself would sound similar to (4c). Conclusion should be drawn after phonetic verification.

6 Here this example of the rise-fall intonation pattern is given tentatively. If this pattern is included, altogether four of them are distinguished in the Japanese intonation contour variation: fall, rise, fall-rise, and rise-fall. I shall preserve the existence of the last one until it is attested more rigidly, however.

7 It is not stated in his Japanese description what this labelling *Pro. L* stands for.

8 The detail of the definitions of these terms are not explicit in Campbell (1997). They are too vague as the linguistic definition.

9 When the author's name is not listed in the bibliography at the end of this paper, the source is Hirst and Di Cristo (eds, 1998a). The titles of the papers are "Intonation in (the name of the

34

targeted language)." To take Gibbon (1998) for an example, its title is "Intonation in German." in Hirst and Di Cristo (eds., 1998a).

10 He cites the following work as the source, though the detail in the original paper simplified: Pheby, J. (1975) *Intonation und Grammar im Deutschen*. Berlin: Akademie-Verlag.

11 Halliday (1967a, 1970) exemplifies the intonation patterns and the meaning, practical nuances denoted by them of British English.

12 't Hart (1998: 101) clarifies the definition of hat pattern as 'a typical pattern for the intonation of a short non-emphatic declarative phrase in Dutch.'

13 In the examples are retained capitals indicating stress fallen on the syllables, preserving the ways in Cruz-Ferreira (1998).

14 Di Cristo (1998) cites the following references by the same author:
Delattre, P. (1966) "Les dix intonation de base du français." *French Review* 40, 1: 1–14.
—— (1967) "la nuance de sens par l'intonation." *French Review* 41, 3: 326–339.

15 Intonation groups are divided by square brackets. These indications of intonation patterns are attached only for the words concerned words in the pair. The labels of intonation patterns *Bottom (Btm), Top* substitute the arrow symbols in Dascălu-Jinga (1998), which bases IN-TSINT (an international transcription system for intonation) as a rough phonetic description of the utterances. For the detail of INTSINT, see Hirst and Di Cristo (1998a: 14–18).

16 Botinis (1998) lists the following references concerning STU:
Bannert, R. (1985) "Toward a model for German Prosody." *Folia Linguistica* XIX.
Brown, G., Currie, K. L. and Kenworthy, J. (1980) *Questions of intonation*. London: Croom Helm.

17 Fónagy (1998) cites the following two references as the basis of his discussion:
Varga, László. (1981) "A magyar intonáció — functionális szempontból. (Hungarian intonation — from a functional point of view)" *Nyelvtudomanyi Közlemények* 83.
——(1983) "Hungarian sentence prosody: An outline." *Folia Linguistica* 17.

18 British and American English is regarded as one language, though Bolinger (1998) and Hirst (1998) are independent chapters in Hirst and Di Cristo (eds, 1998a).

19 The status of Japanese as one of the Altaic languages is not established yet, as I understand it. This is a tentative postulation for the present rubrication.

20 As suggested in section 5, Danish will be an exception to this generalization in the Germanic languages; it should be dubbed as a SIS.

21 Hockett (1958: 34) comments as follows:
It is PERHAPS true that certain features of speech melody are to be found in all languages (e.g., rise of pitch and volume under the stimulus of pain or anger), but such universal features, if they exist, are not part of intonation as we now use that term. Recent research suggests that every language has a system of basic speech melodies which is as unique to the languages as is its set of vowel and consonant phonemes. (emphasis added).

CHAPTER 3

On the Multi-Layer Structure of Metafunctions

3.1 Introduction

'Metafunction' is a major tool of Systemic Functional Linguistics (SFL) in analyses of not only verbal texts but also other genres such as paintings and music. In the present chapter, it will be exemplified how meanings of verbal expressions are analyzed from the viewpoint of metafunctions, partly using intonation as examples.

Metafunctions are divided into three categories in general: Ideational, Interpersonal and Textual. In another viewpoint, one of the three is further classified into two subcategories: Ideational into Experiential and Logical. It is sometimes confusing whether metafunctions consist of three or four domains. One of the major concerns in the present chapter is to pursue the legitimacy of the framework of metafunctions in that it should be considered to consist of three major distinctions, or it should be classified as four subcategories including the subdivision of Experiential and Logical.

First, we will look at an entire picture of the framework of SFL. Below is the figure from the webpage of Professor Emeritus Noboru Yamaguchi at Tohoku University.[1]

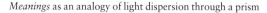

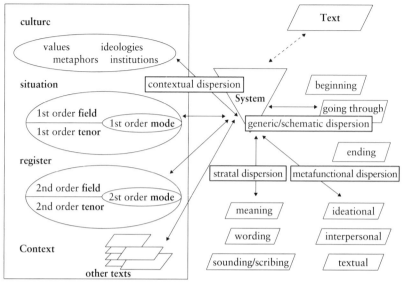

Figure 3.1: Text, system and context

This illustration well depicts how text is analyzed in SFL. A text is considered as input; through a prism — called System in (figure 3.1), as in the name of *Systemic* Linguistics, suggesting the process of selection(s) from input to output —, it is analyzed from various viewpoints of culture, situation, register, strata, and metafunction. Though each of these is depicted as independent stratum in this figure, some of them are linked: e.g. metafunction and situation/register.

The three-layer structure of the three metafunction is what I should like to present in the following sections. In this figure, such layer structure is found not only with metafunctions, but also in strata of meaning — wording — sounding / scribing, and the generic / schematic structure of beginning — going-through — ending. It is not accidental that they consist of three-constituents each; as shown in section 3 below, the three constituents are necessarily related.

Next is another figure from Professor Noboru Yamaguchi's webpage,[2] on the cover of the translation of Halliday (1994) into Japanese (Yamaguchi and Kakehi (2001)). According to this illustration, metafunctions are depicted as part of the SFL frameworks, such as logico-semantic relations, ranks, strata, taxis. In my understanding, these elements are interrelated, hence it would be difficult to show such overlapping in a two-dimension chart.

CHAPTER 3 ON THE MULTI-LAYER STRUCTURE OF METAFUNCTIONS

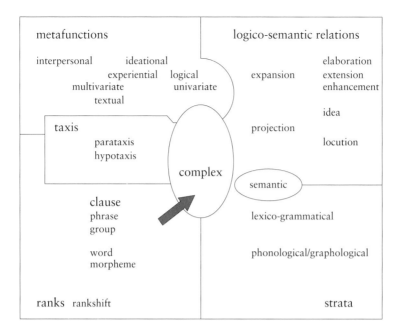

Figure 3.2: Metafunction, logico-semantic relations and lexico-grammatical strata

Partially overlapping with another figure 3.1 in that there shown the relative position of the 'devices,' this picture also visualizes the basic concept of SFL. In this illustration, it is characteristic that *complex* occupies the center position, with other constituents surrounding it.

As for the way how metafunctions are interrelated, the two figures 3.1 and 3.2 differ from one another. In 3.1, the three are completely parallel. In figure 3.2, however, Ideational is divided into Experiential and Logical, and the other two of Interpersonal and Textual are away from the center. It is suggesting that Interpersonal domain is the farthest from *complex*, the center of the mandara. The next to *complex* is Logical component, which is also meaningful. In addition, Logical component is noticed as *univariate* while the others, including Expriential, are multivariate.

In the following sections, the focus will be laid on metafunctions among others, except in section 2 where the idea of an American phonologist Pike will be introduced.

3.2 American Structurism vs. SFL

In this section, a conceptual contrast will be made between American Structur ism and SFL. The main focus will be laid on the comparison of the layers of in tonation system in Pike (1945) and the strata in SFL. Pike (1945) is a study of intonation in American English, one of the earliest references for that subject in the new world.

Pike (1945: 171) illustrates the types of layers of intonation system as con centric circles, which he calls 'an onion.' Considering the fact that this diagram is included in the last section of his monograph, this is the essence of how he recognized the intonation system of American English in terms of one of the fields of linguistics. His approach to intonation system seems to be a typical product of American Structurism in those days. It is common with the idea of the triplet concentric circles of the metafunctions, introduced below, that meanings can be diagrammed as layer structure.

The center of the circles is dubbed as *SOUNDS TYPES AND SEQUENCES (PHONETICS)*, while the most peripheral one being *SPEECH-GRADIENT CHARACTERISTICS*. For the ease of looking each layer horizontally, the ar rangement will be converted into plain listings in the table below. The outer most layer (speech-gradient characteristics) will be put on the first line, and the innermost one being on the last line. For the purpose of reference, the numbers will be assigned to each line, which are not original in Pike (1945). Typography of capital letters is maintained.

(1)

1. SPEECH-GRADIENT CHARACTERISTICS
2. SUPERIMPOSED ON LINEAR STRUCTURE
3. AGE AND SEX CHARACTERISTICS
4. Personal Differences
5. General Quality of Harshness, Resonance etc. from Articulation, Set of Throat, Vocal Cords, Lips, Tongue, Lungs
6. General Modification of Key, Pitch Gap, Rate, Loudness, Abruptness, Crescendo, Decrescendo
7. General Type of Utterance — Song, Whisper, Speech Aloud, Falsetto
8. LINGUISTIC STRUCTURE—SYSTEMATIC CONTRASTS
9. SUPERIMPOSED ON LINEAR STRUCTURE
10. Contrasts of Rhythm, Pause and Sentence Stress
11. Intonation Contours with Internal Structure
12. Four Contrastive Pitch Levels
13. LINEAR STRUCTURE
14. Words and Intricate Structure of Sequences of Words (Syntax)

CHAPTER 3   ON THE MULTI-LAYER STRUCTURE OF METAFUNCTIONS   39

15. Morphemes and Intricate Structure of Sequences of Morphemes
(Morphology)
16. Phonemes and Intricate Structure of Sequences of Phonemes (Phonology)
17. SOUND TYPES AND SEQUENCES (PHONETICS)

It seems at the first glance at the original diagram in Pike (1945:171) that different kinds of items are mixed in the listing: i.e., headings, notes and contents. Before analyzing the items and contrasting them with the SFL strata, the mixture should be reorganized.

The first key, it seems, to decipher this complicated listing is the distinction of those lines in capital letters and those in normal ways. The capital-letter lines are for indicating the headings or titles, or notes. The other lines are the inventories under the headings. To take an example from the third and fourth lines; AGE AND SEX CHARACTERISTICS (line 3) are equivalent to Personal Differences (line 4).

The second key is the repetition of the note-like comments of LINEAR STRUCTURE or SUPERIMPOSED ON LINEAR STRUCTURE. These comments appear in lines 2, 9, and 13. The first line (SPEECH-GRADIENT CHARACTERISTICS) is the general title for this diagram, for example. The repetition of the note-like comments may suggest that these 17 lines of layers can be classified into three groups: lines 2 through 7, 8 through 12, and 13 through 17. The listing of the first group represents phonetic features, whereas that of the second one lists phonological elements. The last group contains the four sections of linguistics.

Whereas the first two notes in the lines 2 and 9 are SUPERIMPOSED ON LINEAR STRUCTURE, the last one is only LINEAR STRUCTURE, without SUPERIMPOSED ON. This implies that line 13 contains four fields of linguistics: syntax, morphology, phonology, and phonetics. These four sections were ALL of the linguistics at that time, when semantics and pragmatics had been outside of the concern of linguists. Hence, the first two groups had to be something that were added on the basis of the major four departments of linguistics.

As is clear from the parenthesized four classification of syntax, morphology, phonology and phonetics, this arrangement is based on the 'tradition' of American Structurism. That is to say, the first step to investigate a given language is phonetics in the sense that human speech sound is a physical entity; hence we can depend on a methodology in phonetics which is close to natural science. As the next step, such speech sounds are classified and analyzed in the framework of phonology. In a broad sense, both phonetics and phonology deal spoken language. Contrastively, morphology and syntax are not confined to spoken mode. In the American Structurism tradition, linguistics had been assumed to pursue these four sections. That means 'meaning' had been excluded from the main stream of that school.

Those inner layers assumed by Pike will partly correspond to the Lexico-grammatical and Phonological strata within the SFL scheme. The division of phonetics, phonology, and so on, in the Structurism tradition corresponds with the strata in the Systemic terminology. In my understanding, the correspondence between the two frameworks will be as follows:

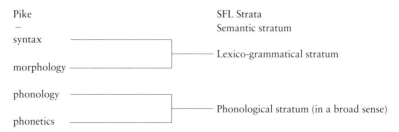

Figure 3.3: Structurism and SFL

It will be understood that phonology within the SFL scheme include the sphere of phonetics as indicated by my note 'in a broad sense' in the parenthesis. Syntax and morphology in the Structurism tradition are integrated into Lexico-grammatical stratum in the Systemic Linguistics. Generally, the terminology and classification are simpler in SFL than in American Structurism.

The Semantic stratum of the SFL scheme is not able to find its counterpart in Pike's circles. This is because the Structurism linguists, including Pike, did not reach the realm to pursue the domain of semantics and above. Hence now, we must stop the direct comparison of the frameworks between American Structurism and SFL.

My revised version for Pike's illustration is a three-dimensional one, maintaining the concentric circle structure. One of the major purposes of this revision is to eliminate the overlap of the phonetic features in the first group and the phonological elements of the second group, both of which are included in the domains of phonetics and phonology of the third group. Another aim of this re-illustration is the literal realization of the notion 'SUPERIMPOSED ON LINEAR STRUCTURE.' In order to picturize the superimposition, three-dimensional concept is necessary. Thus, the concentric circles have turned into three layers, with the headings thrown out of the circles. The size of the circles are differentiated so that the first one should be largest, and the last one smallest. The capital-letter lines are remained as such except the last line (PHONETICS), each heading being shortened for the sake of simplicity.

CHAPTER 3 ON THE MULTI-LAYER STRUCTURE OF METAFUNCTIONS

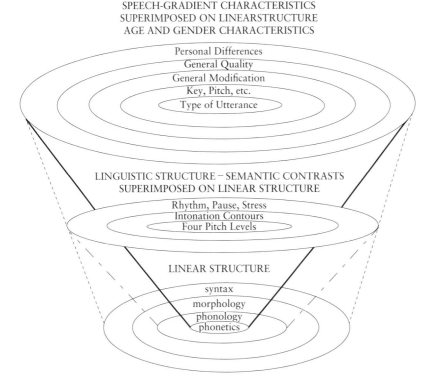

Figure 3.4: Pike's onion model

With this demonstration, Pike's intention has become clarified; more detail — those items in the first two layers — is given for phonetics and phonology than for syntax and morphology among the four sections, since this framework is based on the study of intonation in Pike (1945). The first layer is reflected on the phonetic domain of the LINEAR STRUCTURE, and the second circle is projected on the phonology counterpart. It is interesting that the phonetic features are extraposed on the top of the triplet circles, which can be considered as the outermost on the one hand, and the innermost concentric circle of LINEAR STRUCTURE on the other. Phonological component occupies the middle position in two-fold sense: of the three layers, it is the second one, and in the four-section LINEAR STRUCTURE, it is located in the inner one together with the morphology domain.

To summarize; in American Structurism, each of the strata (in the SFL sense) — i.e. phonetics, phonology, morphology and syntax — is inorganically separated, and the pursuit of the interrelationship between these sections is rare.

This observation can be typified, at least in Pike (1945), that interpersonal and textual perspective can not be found between the lines. This is not to deny, however, the scholastic value of Structurism; it is just to point out the methodological difference between formalism in the Structurist tradition and Halliday's functionalism. Historically it is ascertained that American Structurism had not taken semantics and beyond into account. Bolinger (1986, 1989) is in line with such Structurism approach in that though phonetic details are given for intonation system of American English, and that few semantic analyses are given.

3.3 The Definition of Three Metafunctions

In this section, various aspects of the SFL explanation are contrasted with regard to three metafunctions. Among them, Halliday (1979/2002) is one of the most important and the earliest references when discussing the meaning and function of metafunctions.

First, let us briefly review the history of the terminology. It was in Halliday (1970) that the concepts first appeared in the literature. The triplet ideational, interpersonal and textual was established at that time, but the terms for these three was *function* and *meaning potential*. (Halliday (1970/2002: 174-175)). In 1973 the rubric was changed into *macro-function*, maintaining the framework of the triplet. One of the triad, i.e. Ideational metafunction, is replaced by *Experiential* in the 1974 publication (Halliday (1974)), which will be suggestive in the discussion of the statuses of Ideational, Experiential and Logical domains in next section. These were dubbed as merely *function* at that time. Then, in Halliday (1979) these frameworks had been developed to greater extent, again using the term *meaning potential* (Halliday (1979/2002: 198)). Halliday (1985a) used the term *metafunction* instead of *macro-function*. In the present chapter, *metafunction* will be solely adopted.

Now here is an introductory sketch with concise definitions in chapter 2 of Halliday (1994). Below is a sketchy table where various aspects concerning three metafunctions are woven into.

Table 3.1: Metafunctions

Metafunction	Paraphrase	Structure	Others
Ideational	Clause as Representation	Process	
Interpersonal	Clause as Exchange	Mood + Residue	Polarity, Modality
Textual	Clause as Message	Theme+Rheme, Old+New Information	

Ideational Processes include the following six: Material, Mental, Relational, Behavioural, Verbal, Existential. The items of the column 'Paraphrase' represent the titles of chapters 3, 4 and 5 of Halliday (1994), respectively. These headings represent what the three metafunctions stand for. Later in the concluding section, this table will be enlarged so that more comprehensive picture of the three metafunctions be presented.

Before pursuing new images of metafunctions, we will briefly review how they have been explicated. It seems that Halliday (1979/2002:217) most concisely summarizes the difference of the three metafunctions:

(2) ... ideational meanings reflect the *field* of social action, interpersonal meanings reflect the *tenor* of social relationships and textual meanings reflect the *mode* of operation of the language within the situation. (italics added)

The triplet terms *field, tenor* and *mode* constitute the three elements of context of situation, which is another important framework of SFL. This triplet set of the elements of context of situation is parallel to the three metafunctions within the internal domain of linguistics. As the terms show themselves, *context of situation* lies outside the domain represented by metafunctions. Halliday (1985b:2002: 284) contrasts these two facets as *Situation* and *Lexicogrammar*. Here the relationship between the two aspects will be diagrammed as below:

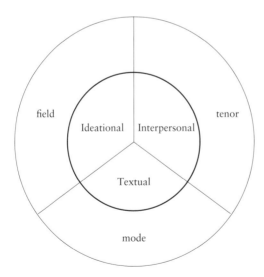

Figure 3.5: Situation and lixicogrammar

The double-layer structure of this illustration comes from the necessity of depicting the relationship between metafunctions and context of situation:

44

metafunction is a concept based on the internal function of language, whereas context of situation is rather *meta*linguistic. It follows then that the equal division of one circle into three parts is different from the *un*equal positioning in concentric circles for metafunction for intonation to appear in (16) in the next section. It is not appropriate in the present chapter to include the domain of context of situation in considering the framework of conclusive sphere of metafunctions; it will be given to next occasion.

With regard to the preference of the triad correspondence of context of situation and metafunction in figure 3.5, however, it must be emphasized that the scheme of the former is useful for that of metafunction. This three-to-three correspondence is neat *vis-à-vis* a three-to-four version, in which the Ideational domain is divided into two.

More detailed explanation for the three metafunctions is given in Halliday (1981/2002: 230):

(3)   A text is a polyphonic composition of ideational, interpersonal and textual "voices". The ideational voice provides the content: the things, facts and reports; processes, participants and circumstances; the logical relations of different kinds. The interpersonal voice provides the interaction: mood, modality, person, polarity, attitude, comment, key. The textual voice provides the organization: thematic and informational prominence; grammatical and lexical cohesion among the parts. The "character" of the text is its pattern of selections in these various voices, and the way they are combined into a single whole.

In section 6.2. in Halliday (1994), some useful insight in regard to Interpersonal and Textual metafunctions is given, related to intonation. It is strange, however, those comments for Ideational counterpart, parallel to these two, can not be found in that subsection. When the Ideational metafunction is divided into two subcategories of logical and experience, the former includes *things* and *names*, *things* being the title of subsection 6.2.3. of Halliday (1994). Enumerated below are explications for the two metafunctions from 6.2.4.:

(4)   Interpersonal
 · The interpersonal meanings are expressed by the intonation contour.
 · Interpersonal meanings tend to be scattered prosodically.
    Textual
 · ... by the 'Mood' block, which may be repeated as a tag at the end, and by expression of modality which may recur throughout the clause.
 · ... textual meanings tend to be realized by the order in which things occur, and especially by placing of boundaries.

- The textual meaning of the clause is expressed by what is put first (the Theme); by what is phonologically prominent (and tend to be put last — the New, signed by information focus); and by conjunctions and relatives which if present must occur in initial position.

An insightful reference to Pike[3] by Halliday is physical metaphors of the three metafunctions, together with 'abstract' icons of particle, field and wave (Halliday (1979/2002: 209-211)). Here Ideational metafunction is substituted by Experiential.

Table 3.2: Contrast of Pike's imge and Halliday's image

metafunction	Pike's image	Halliday's image
Experiential	particle	elemental
Interpersonal	field	prosodic
Textual	wave	culminative − periodic

The reason is not given in Halliday (1979) why these metaphors are adopted as analogy of metafunctions, though the idea itself seems inspiring. Halliday (1981/2002: 239) comments that 'the details of this interpretation are not quite the same as those worked out by Pike.' Further, it is mystifying that this metaphor is not cited in Halliday (1985, 1994) which are indispensable references in SFL. Halliday's images will be presented in section 6 below, with slight modification from those in Halliday (1981).

As for the Textual analogy to wave, we can refer to Halliday (1981/2002: 233):

(5) In its "textual" aspect, a clause has a wave-like periodic structure created by the tension between theme — rheme (where theme is the prominent element) and given — new (where new is the prominent element); the result is a pattern of diminuendo—crescendo, with a peak of prominence at each end. There is a balance of development (i) away from the theme, and (ii) towards the new.

This can be schematized as below with the excerpt from 'silver text' in Halliday (1994: Appendix 1):

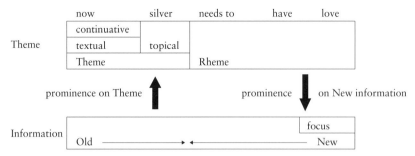

Figure 3.6: Theme and Information structures

In the Theme + Rheme structure, prominence is fallen on Theme and then gradually reduced toward Rheme—a decrescendo pattern described above. Contrastively, Old information is not prominent in general but increasingly heightened as New Information toward the end of the utterance, which is a case of crescendo. With these two prominent heights at both ends, each utterance is provided with boundaries by Textual metafunction.

Now we are ready to discuss the Experiential and Logical subdomains. Halliday (1994:36, table 2(3) in chapter 2) summarizes the Experiential and Logical components as follows:

(6)   Definition (kind of meaning)   Favoured type of structure
   experiential construing a model of experience segmental (based on
                                                   constituency)
   logical   constructing logical relations   iterative

These definitions are, however, tautological and seem to lack in substantial explanation. The only suggestion by Halliday himself, though omitted in (6) above, is the item for 'Corresponding status of clause'; for the Experiential component, the heading 'clause as representation' is given, but none for the Logical counterpart. It will lead to an assumption that Experiential metafunction is more important to represent the Ideational component than Logical, at least as parallel status to Interpersonal metafunction as 'clause as exchange' and Textual as 'clause as message.' As a conclusion drawn from a brief review here, experiential component is partially equivalent to Ideational metafunction. This is fortified with the 'historical facts' that the triplet was Experiential, Interpersonal and Textual in Halliday (1974, 1979). Logical component occupies relatively smaller portion.

Now, let us think about the order of context of situation and metafunctions. The origin of context of situation dates back to 1964 when Halliday, McIntosh

CHAPTER 3 ON THE MULTI-LAYER STRUCTURE OF METAFUNCTIONS   47

and Strevens wrote about the three aspects of field, tenor and mode. That of metafunctions is Halliday (1970), as far as I can tell. Then, it would be natural to assume that each metafunction corresponds to field, tenor and mode respectively. It was later, maybe in Halliday (1979), that Ideational domain was divided into two subcategories of Experiential and Logical.

There is one insightful remark for the source of each metafunction in Halliday (2002: 311). SFL owes its background to the following predecessors:

(7) Ideational: Boas, Sapir, Whorf
     Interpersonal: Malinowski, Firth
     Textual: Mathesius, Prague school

It is interesting in that though the three metafunctions are unified triplet, each source is diversified. It will be another topic to investigate and contrast these sources.

3.4 The Concentric Structure of Three Metafunctions in Intonation

When considering the 'meaning' of the text, whether it is spoken or written, the three metafunctions are more important than other schema depicted in (2), such as Taxis, Ranks, and Strata. Taxis is a systemic selection of 'syntactic' nature. Rank is a distinction of 'length' of linguistic unit: morpheme, word, group, phrase and clause. Strata correspond to the 'traditional' section of phonetics, phonology, morphology, syntax, semantics and pragmatics.

In this section, it will be examined that the three metafunctions are directly related to intonation. Notice that the discussion in sections 4 and 5 is on the meaning conveyed by Key of the intonation patterns. It must be distinguished from those structures of Process related to Ideational metafunction, Mood + Residue of Interpersonal metafunction, Theme + Rheme and Old + New Information of Textual metafunction. They are inherent to the text itself, not to intonation. In later sections, some amendment will be added to the SFL scheme considering the result attained from such discussion.

First, the domain of intonation. My hypothesis on the layer structure of the three metafunction can be illustrated as the triplet concentric circles, as far as meaning conveyed by intonation is concerned (see the discussion below and the diagram). Ideational metafunction is divided into two subcategories of logical and experiential components with dotted line, the size being similar to each other in spite of a brief review of these two subcategories in section 3 above:

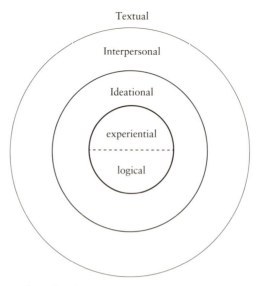

Figure 3.7: Structure of metafunctions

Now let us examine whether this order of the three metafunctions fit into reality or not. The following definition of the three metafunctions is intended only for those meaning conveyed by intonation. More 'authentic,' or close-to-the-physical-world definition will be given in next section.

Ideational metafunction should be innermost in the sense that this domain is concerned with 'what is said' in the utterance, hence it forms the core of the text. Both Interpersonal and Textual metafunctions are based on the content of Ideational domain, with the presupposition in the Experiential and/or Logical subcategories. In other words, the meaning and/or nuance related to these two metafunctions presuppose the logical reality manifested by Ideational department. To put it in still other way, Interpersonal and Textual meaning/nuance is added on the basis of the content of Ideational metafunction.

To be more concrete; Interpersonal metafunction deals with the aspects of 'who said something to whom.' In this expression, *something* is dealt with Ideational metafunction, and the relationship between the speaker and the hearer is controlled by Interpersonal department. Textual metafunction works in such a direction as to make the text coherent. Such Textual metafunction is completed either within one clause, or across the boundaries of single clauses. Tone concord, tone sequence, paratone are the examples of Textual metafunction in intonation (Section 10 in Chapter 8 (Halliday 1994) is devoted to the first two phenomena of tone concord and tone sequence. See Wennerstrom (2001) for paratone). Both tone concord and tone sequence are self-conclusive within one

CHAPTER 3   ON THE MULTI-LAYER STRUCTURE OF METAFUNCTIONS   49

clause, while paratone should necessarily go beyond the borders of clauses. If there is no necessity of the text to be coherent — for instance, it is short enough to be understood immediately — Textual metafunction can be optional.

If the order of the metafunctions were reversed, one of the possibilities were the case in which Textual were the innermost and hence most substantial. If so, where would be the *content* of the text? As exemplified in the paragraph just above, Textual metafunction is optional and indispensable as at least the Ideational domain as is necessary for the linguistic world. Ideational content is indispensable in any text, on the other hand. As a conclusion, this reverse order is impossible at all.

Another possibility would be that Interpersonal were the core of the concentric circles. In that case, the same question would be effective as counterevidence. When contrasting the importance of Interpersonal and Ideational metafunctions with regard to the core content, again Ideational should be positioned more centralized. Interpersonal division is subsidiary to the Ideational metafunction as what makes a text meaningful. It has become evident through these examinations that the text must have some logical reality that can be judged either true or false. As a result, Ideational metafunction should occupy the innermost position.

One of the reasons why Ideational domain must evaluated as the core may be that it is divided into two subcategories of Experiential and Logical. If the content in the Ideational domain were not abundant, it could not be plausible to divide it into more minute subdomains.

The next step to investigate the order of the three metafunctions is that between Interpersonal and Textual metafunctions. It should be concluded that Interpersonal must be positioned more interior than Textual counterpart. The reason is that any text cannot be existent without interpersonal relation; there must be speaker or writer, and hearer(s) or reader(s), whereas it can go without Textual organizations in the sense that there is no indispensable elements such as the logical content of the Ideational domain and the participants in Interpersonal metafunction. Notice that Processes, realization of Textual metafunction and the topic of Chapter 5 in Halliday (1994), is now outside of the current discussion. Here those related to Textual metafunction must be interpreted as something that makes text coherent.

Notice that this triple concentric circle is intended to exemplify the meaning structure INHERENT TO INTONATION. That is to say, individual metafunctional systems are not included in the consideration in figure 3.8 such as Process for Ideational, Mood + Residue structure for Interpersonal, Theme + Rheme structure and Old + New information. Hence, there will be no resemblance between figure 3.8 and the one like figure 3.5, though both are visualized with circles.

3.5 New Images of Metafunction

Following the lines done for the revision of Pike's concentric circles of intonation system in section 2, let us draw again a picture of the three metafunctions, taking the meaning conveyed by intonation into an account as well as the three layers of metafunctions. This time, the sizes of the circles are equalized, since it is not necessary to imitate Pike's onion model (5), in which the sizes of the three circles are differentiated.

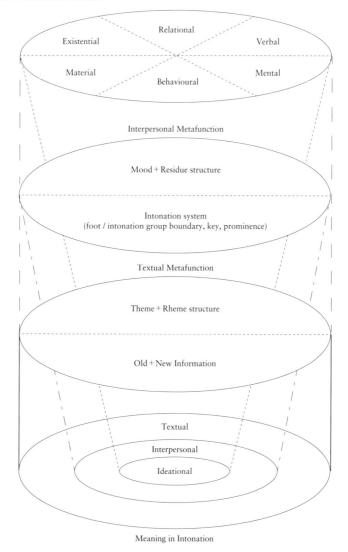

Figure 3.8: Six processes in ideational metafunction

CHAPTER 3 ON THE MULTI-LAYER STRUCTURE OF METAFUNCTIONS 51

In a sense, this three-dimensional chart can be converted into a 'ordinary' two-dimensional table such as Figure 13 in Halliday (1979/2002: 211), apart from the basement concentric circle in which three metafunctions are put together. Here Ideational component is NOT divided into logical and experiential subcategories for the sake of simplicity of the illustration.

As for the lines connecting those circles of the upper three and the inner or outer smaller ones in the bottom, some verbal supplement would be necessary.

First, the Ideational sphere. The selection from the six Process types is projected to the Ideational domain, which occupies the innermost circle at the bottom. This means that in any utterance, content should be classified into any of the six Process types, since these six Processes are mutually exclusive. In other words, these six Processes make a system network. In what is related to intonation, the Ideational metafunction makes the core of the utterance: what is manifested verbally.

The second circle is concerned with the Mood + Residue structure, the system related to the Interpersonal metafunction. In Tench (1996:20)'s expression, this metafunction reflects '[n]ot what they said, but the way they said it.' This 'way' will include those facets concerned with Textual metafunction. The Interpersonal layer is reflected to the domain sandwiched between Ideational and Textual metafunctions at the bottom concentric circle. It means that Interpersonal metafunction is positioned as the middle of the three; it always comes between Ideational and Textual metafunctions. Interpersonal nuances, defined in Kadooka (2001a, b), is directly concerned with this domain. When it is necessary to take intonation into consideration, those aspects must be added to this sphere such as foot / intonation group boundary, key and prominence.

The Textual layer consists of the two system structures of Theme + Rheme and Old + New information. Since its counterpart at the basement circle is outermost, the lines linking these two domains are 'straightforward' or vertical. One of the missions of the Textual metafunction is to mark the boundaries in the utterances. Typically, and unmarkedly, the utterance-initial position is simultaneously marked with Theme/Old information, whereas the terminal position is realized by Rheme/New information.[4] Both Theme and New information, when realized in the clause-final positions, receive phonological prominence. This job of making a text ordered is indicated as the outermost position of the three metafunctions.

As for the first three layers, multi-dimensional analyses have been made adopting all the methods listed above for the same text: for example, an analysis for 'the silver text' in Appendix 1 in Halliday (1994). In proportion with the three layers of metafunction, such structure was depicted as the overlapping three circles in figure 3.7. It should be emphasized here that the concentric circle of the basement is additional to these triplet set of framework.

3.6 Text Analysis: An Example

In this section, we will analyze a one-utterance text as a case study, taken from Halliday (1979), with the metafunction framework and the emphasis on intonation at the same time. The purpose of these analyses is to investigate how similar, or how different, are the meaning structures within and outside the domain of intonation. If the two dimensions of the structure are similar, a four-layer illustration such as figure 3.7 is unnecessary; if they are dissimilar to each other, then, to examine how different is the next step of the research.

Below is the example from Halliday (1979/2002: 210-211), with the intonation transcription:[5]

(8) //4 ∧ on / **Sunday** per//1 haps we'll / take the / children to the / **circus** // 2 **shall** we//

This utterance consists of three tone groups, separated by double slashes. The first tone is realized as a fall-rise with the prominence on *Sunday*, indicated by bold type. The second group consists of four feet distinguished with single slashes, the prominence fallen on the last word *circus* with the falling tone. The third tone group is a tag question *shall we*, with the steep rise Tone 2 toward the end of the whole utterance.

In Halliday's interpretation, intonation is almost exclusively related to Interpersonal metafunction. Another domain of interpersonal nature is Modality/Mood; in the example above, *perhaps* carries Modality, and *we'll* is Mood, in which *we* is Subject and *will* (*'ll*) is Finite. It must be noticeable that the foot boundaries are inconsistent with these Modality/Mood structure. A Modality adverb *perhaps*, for example, is divided into two feet, the first syllable belonging to the first tone group while the second syllable to the second group. This is because of the regulation of foot structure that the first syllable of a given tone group must be either a stressed syllable or a silent beat indicated by a caret (∧).

The most enigmatic point at the moment is what the 'field'-like structure looks like; intonation contour in Figure 3.9 in Halliday (1979/2002: 210) is a line of Fo frequency signifying the movement of the voice pitch, and does not look like a two-dimensional 'field.' From the beginning of this modeling, hinted by Pike's work, this kind of analogy does not have to be logically strict. In other words, we can freely draw pictures to represent the images we have in mind.

Below is the realization of the multi-layer picture of three metafunctions, based on the images of each domain in Halliday (1979/2002: 210). In the Interpersonal sphere, transcription of intonation pattern is adopted with key, tonic and boundaries of feet and intonation groups, instead of intonation contour.

CHAPTER 3 ON THE MULTI-LAYER STRUCTURE OF METAFUNCTIONS

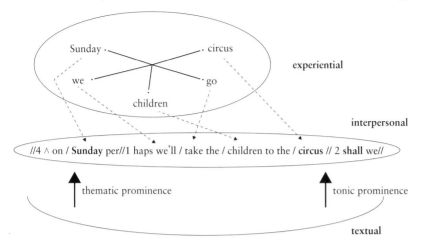

Figure 3.9: A text analysis

With this multi-layer interpretation, it is well demonstrated how each word is realized in each layer and how it is related to each other across the layer boundaries. The five 'particles' in Experiential domain are linked to the corresponding lexical item in the intonation transcription in Interpersonal metafunction. The arrows of the two prominent peaks in Textual domain point to the tonic syllables in Interpersonal sphere. Thus, it is intuitively understood from this illustration that the three layers are organically related to each other, and that they form one text as *meaning potential*.

Next is the reorganization of Figure 3.10 in Halliday (1979/2002: 211) into a similar multi-layer model.

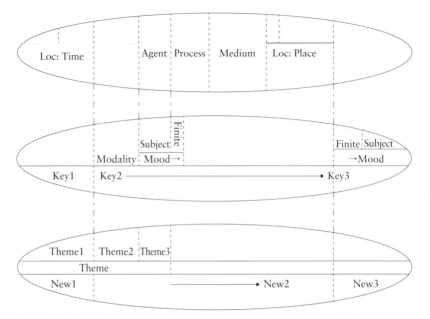

//4 ∧ on / **Sunday** per//1 haps we'll/take the / children to the / **circus** // 2 **shall** we//

Figure 3.10: Another text analysis

Keys 1 through 3 in Interpersonal domain is another tag for intonation groups, focusing on speaker's mental attitude. Key 1 in this case is the first tone group with a fall-rise Tone 4, Key 2 is the second tone group of Tone 1 falling tone, and Key 3 is realized as rising Tone 2.

Exceptional to the canonical information structure is that the first phrase *on Sunday* is not an Old information, but a New one. This is not a crucial violation of basic ordering in the information structure, because there are many exceptions like this. In other words, it is not an inviolable regulation that all clauses must be initiated with Old information. This is further endorsed indirectly with the fact that the violation to the thematic structure is fatal, at least for English, that Theme should be the first element in the utterance or the text.

The change from the two-dimension original table into a three-dimensional one figure 3.10 is virtually nothing. This is because the comparison across the layers is possible with box tables like Figure 3.10 in Halliday (1979/2002: 211). In comparing figure 3.9 and figure 3.10, however, the former is more fruitful in that the individual pictures are meaningfully linked together to make the relation of each layer explicit.

The last diagram in this section is a concentric triplet circle of intonation meaning. Before that, we need the context of situation for the text (8). Let us postulate that this utterance is made by one of the parents to another suggesting to take their children to circus. The date of the utterance will be a few days before the intended Sunday. Then the drawing is like this:

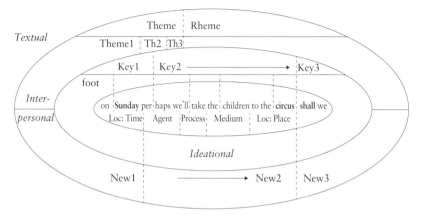

Figure 3.11: The third pattern of the text analysis

Textual metafunction is the outermost circle, divided into two spheres of the Theme + Rheme structure on the upper half and the information structure in the lower counterpart. Interpersonal domain occupies the middle circle, and it is further separated into feet and tone group boundaries. Ideational metafunction is indicated as the innermost circle. This concentric diagram is superior to the box table in that two Textual structure can be presented with two ways of separation patterns; in (3.11) the thematic structure and the information structure are separated to upper and lower ways, and both can be equally parallel to Interpersonal metafunction.

When comparing (3.10) and (3.11), the latter seems preferable in that the three metafunctions are closely linked to each other. In (3.11), each layer is independent, since the circles are distant to each other.

In chapter 8, section 10 in Halliday (1994), tone sequence 1–4 is defined as hypotaxis. In the above text, Tone 2 is added as a tag question following the tone sequence 1–4. A typical realization of hypotactic relation is exemplified with an example as follows:

(9) //4 ∧ as / soon / as she'd / packed her/ **bags** she //1 left / **home** //

When compared with a typical hypotaxis like this, *on Sunday* in (8), only referring to a certain date, the hypotactic relation is weaker.

3.7 Concluding Remarks

So far, we have pursued how metafunctions must take their stand in the SFL scheme. In the course of discussion, it was found that Pike's analysis for intonation structure looks similar to the multi-layer picture of metafunctions. This implies that human language can be methodologically analyzed similarly, across the boundaries of linguistic schools.

As a part of summary of the present chapter, an enlarged version of a table of three metafunctions is presented below:

Table 3.3: Metafunctions by definitions

	Ideational	Interpersonal	Textual
source	Boas, Sapir, Whorf	Malinowski, Firth	Mathesius, Prague school
context of situation	field	tenor	mode
subdomain	Experiential / Logical	—	—
Halliday 1981	things, facts, reports, processes, participants, circumstances, logical relations	mood, modality, person, polarity, attitude, comment, key	prominence, cohesion
Pike's analogy	particle	field	wave
Halliday's analogy	elemental	prosodic	culminative/periodic

Notes

1 The reprinting of the figure, together with the figure ③ below, is permitted by Professor Yamaguchi. I hereby express my cordial gratitude for this reprinting. The URL to see this figure is: http://www.intcul.tohoku.ac.jp/~yamaguch/systemic_room_supplement/sft_profile/text_system_context.html

2 The URL for this figure on line:
http://www.intcul.tohoku.ac.jp/~yamaguch/systemic_room_supplement/semiotics_of?complexing.html

3 Pike, Kenneth L. (1959) 'Language as particle, wave and field.' *Texas Quarterly* 2.

4 Figure 9 in Halliday (1979/2002: 208) appropriately presents this combination of the Theme + Rheme structure and Old + New information.

5 For details of intonation transcription, refer to Halliday (1967a, 1970, 1979/2002), for example. Here the minimum explanation will be given.

CHAPTER 4

English Intonation System as Interpersonal Embodiment

4.1 Introduction

This chapter is an acoustic analysis of the Punch Line Paratone observed as a discourse intonation pattern. The punch line paratone is suggested in Kadooka (2009, 2011a, 2011b) as a subtype of the Low Paratone. Phonetically, the punch line paratone shares the following six observations with the Low Paratone (Tench (1996: 24), emphasis by the present author):

(1) 1. The high pitch on the onset syllable of the initial intonation unit.
  2. The *relatively* high 'baseline' of that initial unit; this means that the low pitches are relatively high, compared to the low pitches in the final unit of the paragraph.
  3. There is a gradual lowering of that baseline until the final unit is reached.
  4. The depth of fall in the final unit is the lowest in the whole paragraph.
  5. There is *usually* a slowing down process in the final unit.
  6. There is a longer pause than is normally allowed between intonation units.

Let us label these with shorter headings as follows; each one corresponding with those above:

(2) 1. high in the beginning
  2. high baseline
  3. gradual lowering
  4. lowest fall before the final
  5. slower tempo in the final
  6. longer pause before the final

In the sections below, we will use these headings. Of these six, *the baseline* of the second statement is slightly ambiguous. That is to say, *the baseline* of an intonation unit seems to indicate a level line of the pitch contour. In any case, the baseline of an intonation unit must be clearly defined. Given the restricted length of this chapter, detailed discussion will be given on a later occasion.

The emphasized two adverbs *relatively* and *usually* are considered to be ambiguators or obscurers in the sense that they do not define something absolutely. In other words, the conditions listed in (1) allow some exceptions. When we simplify — somewhat extremely —, the six conditions are modified as follows:

(3) 1. The high pitch on the onset syllable of the initial intonation unit. (the same as in (1))
2. The average pitch in each line is the highest in the initial line.
3. There is a gradual lowering of the average pitch toward the final unit.
4. The average pitch is the lowest in the final unit.
5. The tempo is the slowest in the final line.
6. The pause is the longest before the final line.

The reason for the modification into (3) is that the ambiguousness in (1) may be diminished with these simplified and extreme measures. These extreme figures will be easier to identify than those in (1).

Thus, the purpose of this chapter is to acoustically exemplify whether the relative (1) or the absolute (3) is more suitable for authentic recordings of English jokes. To achieve this purpose, the acoustic analysis software *praat* will be adopted (www.fon.hum.uva.nl/praat). This software is suitable for various phonetic analyses, including pitch change and duration.

As a general discourse structure, jokes are defined as follows:

(4) 1. Basically, jokes are told as a dialogue between two people.
2. The dialogue starts with a high tone of voice, which signals the beginning of the story.
3. The baseline of the tone of voice is gradually lowered toward the punch line.
4. Before the punch line, there must be a short pause to signal the end of the story.
5. At the punch line, the tone is the lowest in the whole story.

Of these five illustrations, 2 through 5 are concerned with the intonation pattern — especially the pitch variation.

4.2 English Intonation System

The whole system of English intonation appears extremely complicated when one looks at a system network in Halliday (1967a: Appendix). The final output variations are seven patterns of five simple and two compound tones, but the selections to reach these ends are of great diversity. Further, the results as the final outputs are scattered among the whole table; there are altogether 37 terminals in the table.

The table in Halliday (1967a: Appendix) divides each tone more minutely as *secondary tone system*:

(5) 1→wide, medium, narrow; 2→straight, broken;
     4 & 5→high & low, respectively

For the notion *secondary tone system*, Tench (1996: 74) gives comments as follows:

> The secondary tones do not function, as such, in the organization of information — or, for that matter, in either grammar or the communicative functions. Their role is in the expression of attitudes, ...

This description suggests that the secondary tone system is a more appropriate model for indicating interpersonal nuances.

Though the details are not always coincident with that of Halliday's, Watt (1992: 138) subclassifies Tone 1 into four minor groups and glosses each of them for the simple utterance *the police!*:

(6) 1+n: *look out! they're coming!*   1+w: *... that's who!*
     1.: neutral   1—: *... who else*

This subdivision of the falling Tone 1 class is in parallel with the divison of simple Tones 1 through 5 and compound 13, 53; 'what changes is its effect on the dialogue' (Tench 1996: 4).

Chapter 8 in Halliday (1994), however, has abandoned such subclassification, probably due to the space limitation of the volume. It is idiosyncratic there that intonation, together with the rhythm system, is scrutinized in the light of the information structure Given + New. In short, 'tonic foot ... marks where the New element ends' (Halliday 1994: 196).

My point is that there is no holistic and systematic incorporation of the intonation system into the modal system in the current framework of SFL. This will need more consideration in depth, and that would be one of the most suitable examples of the branch of the *Systemic Phonology* (Tench ed., 1992); rather than pursuing phonology by using system networks, the integration of intonation as a phonological system and the interpersonal metafunction will be more worthy of a systemic approach.

4.3 English Tag Questions

There is no exact counterpart in English to the particles in Japanese and Chinese. We can point out that the discourse particles (*DPs*; Schourup (1985) is the first attempt to highlight DPs from the linguistic perspective) such as *you know*, *I mean*, and tag questions in English are functionally and semantically similar to them to some extent. In this section we will examine the similarities and differences between the two systems of tag in English and SFPs in Japanese. The consideration of English DPs will be given to a next opportunity.

Tench (1996: 4) gives an explanation that the tag with the falling pitch 'sounds as if you are pretty sure of your facts': if it is with a rising pitch, 'you will sound as if you are not so sure of your facts.'

English tag clauses convey varied connotations *vis-à-vis* untagged counterparts. Typically they are demanding of consent and confirmation, and less generally information-seeking, which is almost analogous to mere interrogation without tags. The former will be realized with the falling pitch and the latter with the rising tone. Pragmatic background behind the demanding of consent and confirmation is that the speaker knows the answer or the circumstances beforehand.

Below is an instance of the English tag question (quoted from Quirk *et al.* 1985: 1600), with the indication of a rising nucleus (shown with an acute accent) in the main clause followed by a falling nucleus (a grave accent) in the tag[1]:

(7)   She was | looking HÁPpy tonight| | WÀSn't she|

For the untagged version (*she was looking happy tonight*), Quirk *et al.* (1985: 1600) comments as follows:

> This would make it not a question but a polite suggestion that a (confirmatory) comment would be welcome.

In the tagged one, this nuance 'might be expanded' (*op. cit.*, p. 1600).

Halliday (1967a: 26), on the other hand, classifies the tag clauses first by polarity: reversed versus constant. Each pattern is with the examples of Tones 1

CHAPTER 4 ENGLISH INTONATION SYSTEM AS INTERPERSONAL EMBODIMENT 61

and 2, therefore altogether four clauses are demonstrated, including one marked tonality — Tone 1 in polarity constant[2]:

(8) Polarity reversed
   Tone 2: question (neutral) ("I think I know the answer")
   //1 ∧ and in fact / most of the / **Zoo** department were / there //
   2 **weren't** they //
   //1 **Jack's** been here //2 **hasn't** he //

   Tone 1 : demand question ("I know the answer; admit it!")
   //1 —∧ this / isn't quite / **true** //1 — **is** it //
   //1 **Jack's** been here //1 **hasn't** he//

   Polarity constant
   Tone 2: echo statement ("I have just gathered")
   //1 used to be ... the / habit in / **China** //2 **did** it //
   //1 **Jack's** been here //2 **has** he //

   Marked tonality; tag forming one tone group with preceding clause
   Tone 1: echo statement ("I have just learnt"; "I see")
   //1 **Jack's** been here / has he // (*sic*)[3]

These are the simple presentations of the combinations of tones 1/2 and the two polarities, and there is no argumentation on which patterns are marked and which are unmarked. In general, the reversed polarity and tone 1 are unmarked.

In the reversed Polarity Tones 1 and 2, the connotation implied is that 'I know the answer.' Of the two tone variations, the speaker's attitude is more determined with Tone 1; this is in a sense as expected since the rising intonation insinuates uncertainty.

The constant polarity is marked itself. The implication here is that the speaker has just known the fact. If an example of the Polarity constant with Tone 1 falling on the tag foot were included, the system would be 'perfect' in that the possible four combinations would be completed. Instead, the 'missing' one presented above in (8) is the one in which its own tone does not fall in the tag foot.

In Tench's (1996: 38-39) terminology, the reversed polarity is referred to as a *checking tag* and the constant polarity is a *copy tag*. The four versions of the combinations of the polarities and Tone in Tench (1996: 39) are completely congruous to the pattern in (8) above. As to the lack of Tone 1 in copy tag, he notes that 'it will sound distinctly odd.'

Generally speaking, the semantic function of English tag questions and

Japanese SFPs overlap significantly. It would not be accidental that both of the two categories occupy the clause-final positions. The subtler differentiation in meaning is done with the intonation in English, and the choice/combination of particles in Japanese.

To summarize the contents in sections 2 and 3; the expression of the interpersonal nuance in English is undertaken by intonation to a considerable extent, and some with tag questions. In Japanese, on the other hand, it is expressed mainly with the sentence-final particles, which is the topic in the following chapters.

4.4 The SFL Framework

One of the major advantages of SFL is, it seems, that any text can be subject to analysis whether it may be written or spoken. This entails naturally that suprasegmental phonemes such as pitch, stress, and intonation are parallel to syntactic categories such as nouns, adjectives and verbs in that they constitute semiotic code — language — as a whole. In this regard, SFL is quite different from the exclusively syntax-oriented approach to language, represented by that of Chomsky.

Under the SFL framework, languages are considered to be an interacted compound of semiotic code and the culture surrounding it. In those linguistic methodology other than the SFL approach, the similarity might have not been captured between intonation in English and the SFPs in Chinese and Japanese, with regard to the interpersonal nuances.

Under the rubric of *interpersonal metafunction*, those categories belonging to the spoken and the written modes can be contrasted directly. For the more detailed comparison, the framework should be strengthened.

In my understanding, there is one criterion to distinguish semantics from pragmatics; semantics is related in the ideational difference, whereas pragmatics is not. When just examining the instances in this chapter so far, we can see that the distinction between these two approaches is not always clear-cut. The distinction of the case particles *wa/ga* in Japanese, as briefly acknowledged in section 1, is of a syntactic nature in that topic and nominative case is marked respectively; it is pragmatically significant when we face the minimal pair such as (2a) and (2b). In the SFL scheme, such discernment itself is meaningless.

As a matter of fact, however, the SFL framework is constructed upon the English basis. Its typical example is Halliday (1994) in which intonation system is woven into the information structure Given + New. But now that it has been demonstrated so far in this chapter that the interpersonal nuances expressed in English intonation are realized with SFPs in Japanese and Chinese, the grammars of the two languages should be quite different from that of English as depicted in Halliday (1994). The contrast among these three languages will be diagrammed in the next section.

It seems unexpected that the intonation patterns bear various interpersonal nuances in English on the one hand, but it is excluded from the argumentation on the polarity and modality system in Chapter 4 in Halliday (1994). Contemplating that intonation is indispensable in the expressing of interpersonal nuances in the spoken mode, my suggestion is that it should be incorporated into the SFL system.

The strict definition of the *interpersonal nuances* should be elaborated within the Systemic scheme; and to what extent it is valid, the relative position to the ideational and textual metafunctions, and so on.

4.5 English Jokes

We will acoustically analyze four English jokes in this section. These jokes are adopted from Kadooka (2003), which is an English textbook for university and college students, hence the tempo is slower than the natural one, and the pauses between the intonation units are longer than usual. Recordings of these jokes were made by a British speaker.

There are four episodes to be analyzed: *I don't know*, *Discipline*, *Piggy Bank*, and *One Way Street*. The first two are dialogues between the characters, and the other two are not. The latter two are marked in the sense that jokes are basically a conversation between two people.

Below is a table showing the details of the acoustic figures of each story. The first column "ave." is the average frequency of the intonation group; the second one "min." stands for the minimum or the lowest frequency during the intonation group; "max." is the maximum or the highest frequency, and the "range" is the gap between the maximum and the minimum frequencies. All frequencies are indicated with Hertz. "Duration" is indicated by seconds, and "pauses" mean the interval before the line indicated by the second. The lowest figures of the average pitch, the highest through all the intonation units, the narrowest ranges and the longest pauses are emphasized with bold font in the tables. In the second tables, the numbers of words, syllables (σ), the stressed syllables (feet) will be given, together with the duration time divided by each number: i.e. tempo. The largest figures of the duration — i.e. the slowest tempo — will be shown in the bold type.

The first story is the shortest of the four. It is a dialogue between a teacher and a student:

(9) Episode 1: *I don't know.* (7.15 seconds)
  1 Teacher: Tell me three words most commonly used by students.
  2 Student: I don't know.
  3 Teacher: Correct.

line	ave.	min.	max.	range	duration	pause
1	140.74	79.73	204.87	125.14	3.78	
2	214.24	100.79	265.93	165.14	1.09	0.79
3	115.10	104.54	125.21	20.67	0.53	0.81

line	words	tempo	s	tempo	feet	tempo
1	9	0.42	12	0.32	5	0.76
2	3	0.36	3	0.36	2	0.55
3	1	0.53	2	0.27	1	0.53

This first episode is the shortest of the four jokes, consisting of only three turns. The first and the third turns are taken by the teacher, while the second one is taken by the student. The reader intentionally adopts high pitch to imitate the student's younger voice. Most characteristic of this episode is that the punch line consists of only one word: "Correct." In this punch line, the average pitch is the lowest, the range is the narrowest, and the pause before this is longer than the first one between turns 1 and 2. Another point to be mentioned is the tempo of the punch line. When we count the number of the words in each line, the tempo is the slowest in the punch line; one word for 0.53 second against three words for 1.09 second in line 2. But when we count by the number of syllables, two for the punch line against three for line 2. The third possibility is to count the number of stressed syllables, two for line 2 and one for line 3. Still the result with 0.55 second for each stressed syllable in line 2, is slower than 0.53 second in line 3.

The highest pitch through the episode appears in line 2. This is because the speaker imitates the student's young voice, hence it is higher than the counterpart in line 1. This seems to be not in line with the generalization in (1). To be more precise, let us look at the intonation contour:

(10)
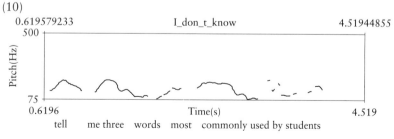

CHAPTER 4 ENGLISH INTONATION SYSTEM AS INTERPERSONAL EMBODIMENT   65

The most prominent word is *commonly*, and the pitch peaks scattering in *tell*, *three*, *commonly* and *used*. When we loosely interpret the generalization in (1), one of the peaks comes in the beginning — hence it is certain that there is a 'high pitch on the onset syllable of the initial intonation unit' ((1) above).

The second episode is a dialogue between a father and his friend.

(11) Episode 2. *Discipline*   (23.24 seconds)
    1. The father was explaining to his friend the difficulty of trying to discipline his son. ↘
    2. "When I was his age, my father sent me to my room for punishment. ↘
    3. But my son has his own TV, CD player and telephone." ↘
    4. "So what do you do?" →
    5. asked the friend. ↘
    6. ⇑ "I send him to **my** room." ↘

line	average	minimum	maximum	range	duration	pause
1	128.49	82.96	182.20	99.24	5.24	
2	124.71	75.88	182.31	106.43	4.45	1.01
3	136.96	78.48	**188.29**	109.81	4.90	1.17
4	157.78	85.84	172.83	86.99	1.17	**1.33**
5	**86.33**	77.26	91.29	**14.03**	0.91	0.00
6	120.82	76.81	176.65	99.84	1.97	1.09

In this example, none of the lowest average pitch, the location of the highest pitch, the narrowest range, the longest pause obey the norms defined in (3) in section 1. The lowest average pitch is realized in line 5; the highest pitch in line 3; the narrowest range in line 5; the longest pause before line 4. The lowest average Fo and the narrowest range appear in line 5, because of the shortness of this line (three words) and the emptiness of the content. These three words are only to signal the speaker of the line, not to present any new information. If we exclude this line from the account of the lowest average Fo considering the latter factor, it is in the last line that the lowest average frequency is realized. The average pause between the lines is 0.92 second. The pause before the punch line is 1.09 seconds, longer than the average.

As for the tonic on *my* in the punch line (line 6), we must look at the Fo diagram:

(12)

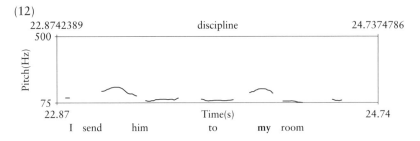

The highest point (176.65 Hz) within this line appears in *send*, not in the tonic *my*. The prominence in this line falls on *my*, not on *send*, however, because the difference must be emphasized between the father's room and the son's room. This distinction by the prominence on *my* is a function of correction of Tone 5 (rise - fall) described in Halliday (1967a, 1970, 1994) and Halliday and Greaves (2008).

The following is a table showing the tempo in each line of this story:

(13)

line	words	tempo	σ	tempo	feet	tempo
1	15	0.35	24	0.22	6	0.87
2	14	0.32	17	0.26	5	0.89
3	11	0.45	16	0.31	4	1.23
4	5	0.23	5	0.23	1	1.17
5	3	0.30	3	0.30	2	0.46
6	6	0.33	6	0.33	2	0.99

When counted by the number of the syllables of each line, it is the slowest in the punch line (0.33 second per syllable in line 6). When counted by those of the words and the stressed syllables, however, it is the slowest in line 3 (0.45 second per word, and 1.23 second per foot). Either way, it is certain that the punch line is told with a slow tempo.

The next one is a dialogue between a mother and a daughter with a narration.

(14) Episode 3: *Piggy Bank*   (30.11 seconds)
    1 Mother decided that her daughter Judy, a nine-year old, was old enough to have her own bank account.
    2 So she took Judy to the local bank.
    3 Judy liked this idea very much.

4 "This is to be your account.
5 You must fill out the application yourself."
6 Judy did well until she came to the space marked, "Name of your former bank."
7 She thought for a while and wrote down,
8 "Piggy."

line	average	minimum	maximum	range	duration	pause
1	123.17	75.06	204.39	129.33	6.65	
2	136.29	94.40	207.45	113.05	2.21	0.70
3	117.19	80.96	192.38	111.42	2.37	1.24
4	126.67	81.20	204.52	123.32	1.81	0.84
5	125.09	89.33	177.20	87.87	2.54	0.57
6	125.45	86.92	199.23	112.31	5.54	1.00
7	115.65	85.15	188.92	103.77	2.90	0.87
8	151.91	82.25	202.41	120.16	0.47	0.40

Below is the pitch contour of lines 7 and 8:

(15)
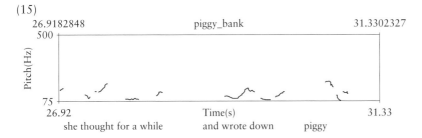

The average frequency in the punch line (151.91 Hz) shows the highest through the story, rather than the lowest. This may be because this line is 'told' by a nine-year old girl — actually she wrote down 'Piggy,' it was not uttered by her. The narrowest range does not appear in the punch line, nor the longest pause before it. The highest pitch appears in the second line, in addition. Thus, this story is exceptional from the standard defined in (3) in section 1. This irregularity may come from the idiosyncrasy that lines 4 and 5 are the mother's turns but Judy does not say anything herself. "Name of your former bank." in line 6 is what is written on the application form, and the punch line "Piggy" is the answer that Judy wrote down on that application form. As an auditory impression of the recording, however, this punch line sounds as if it is uttered by Judy.

The analyses of tempo in this episode is as follows:

(16)

line	words	tempo	σ	tempo	feet	tempo
1	18	0.37	25	0.27	8	0.83
2	8	0.28	10	0.22	2	1.11
3	6	0.40	8	0.30	3	0.79
4	6	0.30	7	0.26	2	0.91
5	7	0.36	11	0.23	3	0.85
6	15	0.37	18	0.31	6	0.92
7	8	0.36	8	0.36	3	0.97
8	1	0.47	2	0.24	1	0.47

The average pause between the lines is 0.80 second, and the pause before the punch line is 0.40 second. Thus, the pause before the punch line is shorter than the average. Though the tempo is the slowest in line 8 when counted by the number of the words, it is line 7 when counted by the numbers of syllables and feet. The reason for this disagreement should be ascribed to the idiosyncrasy of this episode, in that the punch line consists of only one word. Hence the duration per word is the longest in this line, but it is not when counted by the numbers of syllables and feet. As an auditory impression, however, the recording of the punch line sounds slow.

The last episode is the longest one of the four. The whole story is told by narration, including the punch line written on a piece of paper; it is NOT told by a character.

(17) Episode 4: *One Way Street* (36.11 seconds)
1   A Frenchman was visiting New York for the first time in his life.
2   He could not speak English at all.
3   One day he decided to go for a walk.
4   He was afraid of getting lost,
5   so he carefully looked at the street sign in front of his hotel
6   and wrote it down on a piece of paper.
7   He walked around for quite a long time.
8   Then he realized he was lost.
9   He saw a policeman
10   and showed the piece of paper.
11   It said
12   "ONE WAY STREET."

CHAPTER 4 ENGLISH INTONATION SYSTEM AS INTERPERSONAL EMBODIMENT   69

line	average	minimum	maximum	range	duration	pause
1	122.49	92.20	207.86	115.66	4.36	
2	122.74	87.72	156.00	68.28	2.28	0.90
3	140.79	85.00	193.08	108.08	2.48	0.81
4	118.53	78.34	156.19	77.85	1.99	0.90
5	132.07	87.82	204.83	117.01	4.15	0.45
6	124.73	88.34	185.10	96.76	2.24	0.37
7	130.71	75.40	210.59	135.19	2.61	1.38
8	133.05	85.60	196.89	111.29	2.08	1.34
9	138.40	86.80	186.85	100.05	1.22	0.53
10	118.86	91.85	154.57	62.72	1.71	0.41
11	128.25	101.89	176.49	74.60	0.69	1.34
12	117.67	82.18	199.48	117.30	1.38	0.49

The lowest average frequency is found in the last line, which is in line with the ideal pattern of pitch transition. The other factors, however, do not coincide: the highest pitch is in line 7, the narrowest range in line 10, the longest pause before line 7.

This story is an exception to the discourse structure of jokes illustrated in (4) in section 1 in that the whole episode consists of narration, not speeches by the characters. Though there are two characters in this story — namely a Frenchman and a policeman —, neither of them speaks. The punch line "ONE WAY STREET" is what is written on a piece of paper; but still there is a possibility that the police officer read that out.

Below is the pitch contour of lines 11 and 12:

(18)

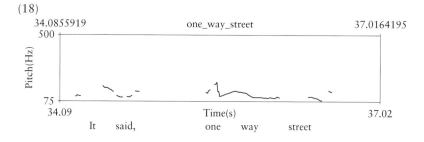

As we see in this picture, line 11 '*It said*' is a fall - rise pattern, while line 12 '*ONE WAY STREET*' is a rise - fall. The tonic of these two lines is on 'ONE' in line 12.

The analyses of tempo is as follows:

(19)

line	words	tempo	s	tempo	feet	tempo
1	13	0.34	16	0.27	5	0.87
2	7	0.33	8	0.29	3	0.76
3	9	0.28	11	0.23	3	0.83
4	6	0.33	8	0.25	2	1.00
5	13	0.32	16	0.26	3	1.38
6	9	0.25	10	0.22	2	1.12
7	8	0.33	9	0.29	2	1.31
8	6	0.35	7	0.30	2	1.04
9	4	0.31	6	0.20	2	0.61
10	6	0.29	7	0.24	2	0.86
11	2	0.35	2	0.35	1	0.69
12	3	0.46	3	0.46	1	1.38

This is the most straightforward result of the four stories analyzed here, all of the three figures coincide in the punch line: the numbers of words, syllables and stressed syllables. The average pause between the lines is 0.81 second, and the pause before the punch line is 0.49 second. Thus, the pause before the punch line is shorter than the average. This is because lines 11 and 12 are to be regarded as one utterance *It said "ONE WAY STREET"* from a syntactic perspective, though they consist of two intonation units. In fact, the pause before line 11 is 1.34 seconds and the second longest with the small difference of 0.04 second to 1.38 seconds before line 7.

Thus, the line-by-line analyses have been done in this section. In next section, the longer analyses across clause boundaries will be done.

4.6 Gradual Lowering

In this section, we will focus on the gradual lowering of the baseline, the third feature pointed out in (1) and (2) in section 1.

The transitions of the average pitch in each episode is as follows:

(20)

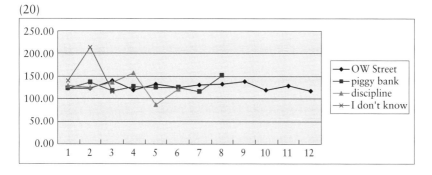

As an observation among the stories, it can be pointed out that the more intonation units a given story contains, the stabler the transition within the story becomes. The most stable pattern is shown with the longest one -- *One Way Street*, while the least stable one is the shortest *I don't know*. The other two come in between these two extremes.

When we extend the transition of the pitch in each story, 'the gradual lowering of the baseline' in (1) 3. above can be paraphrased as follows:

(21) Each story begins with the highest tone of voice of the speaker, and terminates with the lowest tone;
the tone gradually lowers during the story.

To simplify, it would be reasonable in a sense that the second highest pitch is found in the second line, the third in the third line, and so and on. The figure with *One Way Street* would be the nearest to this simplification; this story is told as a narration, not by the characters. In the sense that all the lines are narrated by one speaker, the transition is 'monotonous.'

It may be significant here that the punch line is what has been written on a piece of paper, not told by the Frenchman who can not speak English at all. Though the situation is similar in that the punch lines are narrated and NOT told by the character themselves, the tone of voice is quite different in *Piggy Bank* (10) and in *One Way Street* (13); it is a nine-year old girl who told of herself before the punch line in *Piggy Bank*, but it is an adult male in *One Way Street*.

The reality in other stories is, however, far from this simplification. If the speaker should pretend to be a younger character such as a nine-year old girl in *Piggy Bank* or a student in *I don't know*, the voice must be higher than the ordinary tone. Hence, it is in line 2 in *I don't know* and line 8 or the punch line in *Piggy Bank* that the highest pitches appear. To summarize, the appearance of the highest pitch depends on the discourse structure in the sense that characters such as children and females requiring a higher voice do not always appear in the first line.

When we look at the baseline, or the low pitches instead of the average pitches, what will be the result? Below is the transition of the low pitches of the four episodes:

(22)

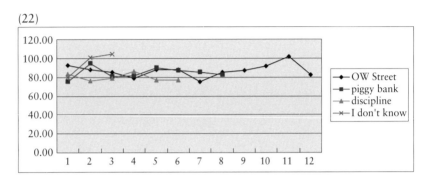

The most probable candidate to satisfy the definition of the gradual lowering may be *Piggy Bank*, when we look at (22). Though the highest pitch is in the second line, we can find a declining tendency toward the eighth line, especially from the fifth line. The changes in *Discipline* are close to this lowering pattern. The other two — *I don't know* and ONE WAY STREET — are, however, NOT close to the generalization of the gradual lowering in (1) and (2). The change in *I don't know* is the opposite of lowering; it is gradual heightening. As pointed out in the previous section, the second line is told as if it were a student; hence the lowest pitch in the second line is higher than that in the first line. As for the changes in ONE WAY STREET, it can be pointed out that there is a lowering in the first half until line 7, but in the second half there is a heightening from line 7 to line 11.

To summarize, it would be difficult to confirm to what extent the generalization of the gradual lowering is applicable, from our examination of the pitch patterns of the four English jokes. One of the main reasons for such exceptions may be idiosyncratic to each story. To take an example in *Piggy Bank*, the punch line 'Piggy' is told by a nine-year old girl. From the phonetic - semantic viewpoint, it seems necessary to define what kind of meaning and function the average and the lowest pitches have.

4.7 Summary

So far, we have looked at the acoustic analyses of some English jokes, with the special focus on the pitch contour and Paratone. In this section, we will concentrate on the topic of which of the two is closer to the truth: the auditory impression of Tench (1) or the extreme acoustic version (3).

Below is a table summarizing the analyses in section 2. The numbers 1, 3, 4, 5, and 6 correspond with those in (1) and (2), and indicated in each cell are those of the episodes which satisfy the conditions:

Table 4.1: Elements of paratone

	(1)	(3)
1. high in the beginning	1, 2, 3, 4	
3. gradual lowering	2, 3, 4	
4. lowest fall before the final	1, 2, 4	1, 4
5. slower tempo in the final	1, 2, 3, 4	1, 2, 3, 4
6. longer pause before the final	1, 2, 4	1, 2

At a first glance, the conclusion would be that the auditory impression in (1) seems superior to its extreme counterpart (3) in that more satisfactory results are given with the former. When counted by the mere numbers of the episodes, 17 with (1) against eight with (3).

Let us examine each item one by one. As for the high beginning, the results are contrastive in that all of the four episodes show agreement with the loose conditions in (1), but none of the four corresponds with (3). The results of the gradual lowering show a similar tendency in that three correspond with (1) but none with (3). With regard to the slower tempo in the final, the results do not differ between (1) and (3); all of the four episodes show agreement both in loose and extreme definitions. The other two — the lowest fall and a longer pause before the final — come between these in that some of those in agreement with (1) are not in (3).

To conclude, the description of Paratone in (1) is quite valid as the result of the acoustic verification of the English jokes. When they are interpreted extremely as in (3), the results are less valid, however.

Kadooka (2011a, 2011b) is a study of Rakugo stories — traditional Japanese funny stories — based on a similar framework to the present chapter. The conclusion there is similar; in the Rakugo stories, there are a fall of the pitch and a longer pause before the punch lines, and the tempo is slower there. The acoustic analyses of the Rakugo stories will reinforce the result given in this chapter.

Notes

1 The notations here are after the one in Quirk et al. (1985): thin verticals are symbols of boundaries of tone units; thick one is the terminal boundaries; nuclei are designated by capitals.

2 The original notation for the nuclei with underlining is substituted with the bold types, following the later modification as in Halliday (1994).

3 It seems strange that Halliday (1967a: 26) introduces this example without the notations of nuclei for the entire utterance. Judging from the preceding comments, it should be indicated as follows:

//1 **Jack's** been here / has he //

4 English DPs are tentatively included in this category, hence its value is designated as ±.

5 The tonality indication with underlining is substituted with italics here.

CHAPTER 5

The Interpersonal-Nuance Carriers in Japanese

5.1 Introduction

In this chapter, we will investigate in which rank scale *interpersonal nuances* are realized in Japanese. The definition of interpersonal nuances is made in Kadooka (1999b), in which the three languages of English, Chinese and Japanese are contrasted within the Hallidayan framework of Systemic Functional Linguistics (Halliday 1994). According to Tench (1996:20), interpersonal nuances reflect '[n]ot what they said, but the way they said it,' which 'refers to the mood of the speaker or the attitude shown to the addressee or the message'. It is typified in Halliday (1967a, 1970) that the English intonation system can reflect speaker's minute mental attitude.

This time, the viewpoint of rank scale will be added, reinforcing the systemic approach to the investigation. Those categories, such as intonation in English and final particles in Chinese and Japanese, which help transmit interpersonal nuances are dubbed as 'interpersonal-nuance carriers.'

The first motive of this study is the finding of the similarity between Japanese particles and English intonation system as interpersonal-nuance carriers. That is to say, both categories are the most eloquent in conveying interpersonal nuances in each language. Then a question arises how to account for this finding in the SFL framework. The present chapter is a step to pursue this challenge.

Before beginning the main discussion, let us establish an assumption as a starting point: interpersonal nuances, or implicit attitude expressed by the speaker, are classified linguistically somewhere in the rank scale. We will now presuppose that interpersonal nuances are the reflections of the pragmatic function of linguistic exchange. The largest purpose of this chapter is to consider whether it is possible or not to regard the different categories of the interpersonal nuance carriers on the unified layer or one of the ranks. We will analyze Japanese for the example.

Another aspect with regard to the SFL scheme is the evaluation of pragmatics apart from the semiotic system. It seems that the concept of 'pragmatics' is not overtly defined in the SFL framework; there is no heading *pragmatic* nor *pragmatics* in the index of Halliday (1994). This would be briefly explicated in the last section of this chapter.

In the next section, the system of rank scale in the SFL scheme will be briefly reviewed. Then later in the following sections, each category of the interpersonal-nuance carriers in Japanese will be looked into one by one: intonation system, phrase final particles (PFP's), case particles and modal auxiliaries.

5.2 Rank Scales in the Semiotic System

In Halliday (1994: 15), the levels of the semiotic system of a language are tripartized: lexicogrammar being the core, with semantics at the higher level and phonology or graphology put below. More precisely, semantics should be referred to as 'discourse semantics' in order to make it explicit that SFL is oriented towards the larger units of speech.

In my understanding, each stratum represents the unit of speech entity subject to linguistic studies. Phonology deals with phonemes and suprasegmentals, graphology is a study of transcribing them to orthographic system; in lexicogrammar words and sentences are analyzed; discourse semantics takes larger text into account.

These three levels are defined with the metaphor of VERTICAL space. Then, one question arises: will this vertical relationship among the three strata lead to the assumption that they do not overlap to each other, and if the borders between them are clearcut. It will be subject to investigation in this chapter whether this verticalization is appropriate or not.

Below is the illustration of this vertical relationship of the three strata (a), contrasted with the *traditional* sectionalism in general understanding (b):

(1) a.

discourse semantics
lexicogrammar
phonology / graphology

b.

semantics
syntax
morphology / lexicology
phonology / graphology

Lexicogrammar being the core of semiotic system in SFL, its counterpart in the non-SFL tradition corresponds to syntax and morphology / lexicology. Though it is depicted in this table that each field in (a) and (b) neatly coincide with its counterpart, actually it does not. It is not a main purpose here, however, to

CHAPTER 5 THE INTERPERSONAL-NUANCE CARRIERS IN JAPANESE   77

point out and pursue such discrepancies. Another problem concerning these tables is that in neither (a) nor (b) it is clear where and how to put pragmatics.

With regard to these illustrations occurs one question: are these mere division of linguistic analyses or some semantic entities? It seems that the latter may be the case since the discussions become a formalistic/methodological matter if the essential consideration is not included as in (b), and only classification is made for the academic sectionalism.

The second question is: if it is the case that semantics and pragmatics must be distinguished in SFL, it will be meaningful that some modification is added to this scheme; another sphere of pragmatics should be juxtaposed to the triad (a). Some conclusion will be drawn in the last section of this chapter.

5.3 Intonation

As Halliday (1970: 21) explicates, '[i]ntonation is one of the many kinds of resources that are available in the language for making meaningful distinctions.' Further he continues that '[i]t is more helpful to think of attitudes and emotions as part of meaning; to consider that all intonation patterns convey meaning, and then ask what kinds of meaning they convey' (*ibid*: 21). To generalize the subcategories of the intonation system, based on Halliday (1970: 22-23):

(2) tone: speech function
    tonic prominence: the structure of information
    mood: kinds of statement, question, etc.
    modality: assessment of the possibility, probability, validity, relevance, etc. of what is being said
    key: speaker's attitude, of politeness, assertiveness, indifference, etc.; all the factors which go to make up the relation between the speaker and the hearer in a speech situation

The English intonation system has been studied as the composite of these subcategories. In the following analysis of Japanese intonation, it is key which is crucial as the interpersonal nuance carrier. It is also key which most suits Tench's comment in Section 1 above.

The Japanese intonation system, on the other hand, has been less systematically integrated into such a multicategorical way, at least as far as I know. Neither concepts nor terms, setting aside the translation and adaptation, is present orderly in Japanese.

In most of the Japanese dialects, the pitch movement is differentiated both in the levels of lexicon and sentence. It is accent in the lexicon, and intonation in longer duration in sentences which are realized as the contour of Fo.

The function of the Japanese intonation system is more restricted than that of English from the semantic and/or pragmatic viewpoint(s). This is because intonation does not function as carrier of interpersonal nuances in Japanese thoroughly. Instead, phrase-final particles (PFPs) play major roles to carry the semantic and pragmatic meaning.

Japanese makes use of the intonation system in the stratum of sentences, though its pragmatic usage is less prevalent than in English. It is similar to English that the declarative and the interrogative are distinguished by intonation. In addition, it is unique in Japanese that interrogative and imperative, or declarative and imperative make minimal pairs. Below is the pair of interrogative and imperative:

(3) a. kore kiru no   (with the rising intonation)
      this wear INTER   'Do I wear this one?'[1]
    b. kore kiru no   (with the falling intonation)
               IMPERATIVE   'Wear this one!'

The contrast shown in Japanese reflects the colloquial and informal situation of the utterances. Of the two, (b) is typically understood as in a situation that the mother is telling her young child to wear a cloth, though the child does not necessarily like it. Such style is seldom adopted for addressing an adult, except between the parties of the extremely intimate relationship such as a husband a wife.

In English, the exactly same kind of contrast of interrogative and imperative is possible, though the word orders are more rigid than in Japanese.

(4) a. Wear this one? (with the rising tone): interrogation
      'Do I/you wear this one?'
    b. Wear this one! (with the falling tone): imperative

(a) is a colloquial echo question uttered in informal situation, and formally it must be supplemented as 'Do I/Do you ...' Such elliptic style conveys the speaker's surprise and/or skepticism. (b) will need no gloss, literally an imperative addressed to one who is in junior position to the speaker.

The contrast between interrogative and imperative kept in the informal and colloquial speech is lost in the formal wording:

(5) a. kore kiru-no   desu-ka?   (with the rising intonation)
            NOMINALIZER COPULA-Q 'Do I wear this one?'

CHAPTER 5 THE INTERPERSONAL-NUANCE CARRIERS IN JAPANESE 79

b. kore ki-nasai   (with the falling intonation)
    IMPERATIVE   'Wear this one!'

The parallelism between an interrogative and an imperative has been lost in (5), which was kept in the less polite and informal version (3). This is partly because the interrogative particle *no* can mostly occur in informal mode while the imperative *no* can not terminate a clause in the formal and polite wording.

It is assumed in Kadooka (2006) that there could be four patterns of intonation in Japanese: fall, rise, fall-rise and rise-fall. The backchannel responses 'soo-desu ka' (Is that so?) and its simplified one-syllable form 'soo' were exemplified as the realization of the four intonation patterns.

This time, other utterance than these backchannel responses will be examined to avoid the repetition and exploit another possibility. Below are the instances of the new example:

(6) a. nan-desu   ka (falling):
        what-COPULA   PFP   'What are you saying?'
     b. nan-desu ka   (rising):
              INTERROGATIVE   'I beg your pardon?'
     c. nan-desu ka: (fall-rise): 'What did you say?; I don't think so."

A *wh*-word 'nan' is a reduced form of 'nani' (what), the two being in complementary distribution in certain circumstances: 'nan' should followed by copula such 'desu' or 'da,' while 'nani' tend to be independent as predicate.

(a) should be interpreted as a cold questioning toward the addressee(s) as if the speaker doesn't care about what had been said or done. The falling tone in this interrogation renders a cold attitude of the speaker. (b), on the other hand, requires the answer by the rising intonation, but the one with falling tone (a) does not necessarily so. Rather, (a) sounds as if the hearer(s) is/are requested further explanation.

In (c), the prominence is fallen on the last syllable *ka:* with the vowel prolonged, reflecting a strong feeling such as surprise and doubt against the speaker's comment by the impressionistic fall-rise tone. Because of this implication with some rudeness, (c) is the most marked pattern of the three.

The rise-fall pattern, is missing from the above listing (6). This tone type is 'the least down-to-earth pattern in the sense that it is too theatrical and hardly heard in the daily situation.' Though it seems that the lack of this pattern in (6) may suggest the weak basis of the existence, we will postpone the conclusion whether it should be included in the intonation pattern inventory in Japanese.

The same kind of the intonation contrast is testified in the one-word clause:

(7) a. nani   (falling intonation):   'What is the matter?'
    b. nani   (rising intonation):   'Pardon me?'
    c. naːni: (fall-rise):   'What did you say?; I don't think so.'

Two simple patterns of falling and rising sound natural, but a complex fall-rise (c) is a little too much emphatic. From the viewpoint of occurrence frequency in natural database, the two simple patterns are predominant while the fall-rise is questionable.

In a sense, it is peculiar with the backchannel response 'soo desu ka' and questioning 'nan desu ka' themselves that are realized with various intonation patterns.

It is now evident that the Japanese intonation system is parallel to that of English as an interpersonal nuance carrier. Its systematicity and the semantic range which it covers is limited, however. In the sense that backchannel responses such as (6) and (7) should be preceded by some statement, the role of the Japanese intonation system is restricted; it can be characterized as passive. Such passive intonation patterns are dubbed as Syntactic intonation systems (SISs) in Kadooka (2001a) *vis-à-vis* more active ones like that of English.

It would be needless to confirm here that the intonation system belongs to the level of phonology. Further, some pragmatic perspective should be added to adapt non-semantic nuances to the SFL scheme in the illustration (1a) in Section 2. Pragmatic aspects as exemplified by intonation in Japanese in this section should be apart from the semiotic three levels of semantics, lexicogrammar and phonology / graphology.

5.4 Final Particles

It is testified in Kadooka (2001a) that Chinese and Japanese are similar to each other in terms of the category and function of the phrase-final particles (PFPs). Below are the examples of the occurrences of phrase-final particles:

(8) Chinese: Zhège   ya,   wǒ xiǎng a,   zhēn hǎo   a,   shì   ba!
         this-one PFP,   I   think PFP truely good   PFP be   PFP
         'This one, I think, is truly good, right?'
    Japanese: Kimi-ne,   hontou-ni ne,   kiyou-da ne!
         you-PFP   truly   PFP   versatile PFP
         'You, I mean, are truly versatile.'

These are the instances of the redundant uses of PFPs, the more 'normal' versions would be as follows:

CHAPTER 5 THE INTERPERSONAL-NUANCE CARRIERS IN JAPANESE 81

(9) Chinese: Wǒ xiǎng zhège shì zhēn hǎo. 'I think this is very good.'
     Japanese: Kimi-wa hontou-ni kiyou-da. 'How versatile you are!'

Roughly speaking, the use of PFPs often entails the change in word orders in Chinese and Japanese.

One of the major differences between Chinese and Japanese is that some of the PFPs in Japanese are interchangeable with interjections, while they are not in Chinese. Below are the examples:

(10) Chinese: Wéi, nǐ ya! *Ba, ǐ ya.
              INTERJ you PFP 'Hey, you!' PFP
     Japanese: Nee, kimi.
              INTERJ you 'Hey, you.'

While PFPs must terminate phrases, interjections should initiate phrases. This gap of the position in the utterance makes contrast in Chinese that the tone of the former category is realized as atonic, but the latter keeps inherent tone of its own, such as the rinsing one in *wéi*.

The Japanese PFPs convey such modal meanings as interrogation, imperative, exclamation, consent and confirmation. Among them, some are concerned with the ideational metafunction: interrogative, imperative, prohibition; others with interpersonal nuances of exclamation, demanding consent, confirmation, attention-calling, and hesitation. Below in this section, we will examine those instances in which such nuances are expressed.

The first category is the clauses of exclamation:

(11) a. kyou-wa ii tenki da naa
        today-TOPIC fine weather AFFIRMATIVE PFP 'How fine it is today!'
     b. How fine it is today!

This type of the emotional announcement is akin to English clauses initiated with *How, What*. Another possible substitute in English is of a phonological nature as in (b): to emphasize with prominence on the modifier, e.g. *very*. In these exclamatory utterances, the messages are self-completed; they can be uttered to the speaker himself/herself, with the intention of talking to no hearer(s). In this sense, interpersonality indicated by exclamatory messages are as weak as those of hesitation utterances.

Next to be examined are demanding consent, and the resembling category of confirmation:

(12) a. soo-da   yo   ne
        right-DECLARATIVE   PFP   PFP   'It's true, isn't it?'
     b. kyou wa   tuitati   dat-ta   ne
        today TOPIC   first day of the month DEC-PAST   PFP
        'It's the first (of the month) today, isn't it?'

As the English translations manifest themselves, these categories of the demanding of consent and confirmation in Japanese are perfectly in agreement with tag questions in English.

For these messages, hearer should talk back to since responses are manifestly required. This is the function of the PFP *ne* to force the hearer(s) to answer to the speaker's question.

The next example is the category of attention-calling, with a particle *yo* parenthesized:

(13) kazi   da   (yo)!
     fire   DEC   PFP   'Fire!'

When it is uttered without *yo*, the statement sounds more serious and urgent. This is because the state of affair requires prompt conveyance of the information. To put it in another way, there would be little room to take interpersonal nuances into consideration in such an urgent situation. When any of the PFPs are attached, the utterance became tedious, as if any serious danger were far away. When no PFP is with the statement, it will be labeled as *zero-PFP*, which is peculiar to the utterances of attention-calling.

As a function of the clauses, it will need no more explanation than the label *attention-calling*. This label *per se* seems to entail strong interpersonal relationship, since the utterances attract addressees' attention. The possibility of the omission of this category of PFPs, however, may be contradictory to this assumption.

The last consideration is on hesitation, or the self-questioning:

(14) dou si-tara   ii-n-darou   nee
     how do-TENTATIVE   well-NOMINAL-FUTURE PFP 'What shall I do?'

The English translation is with the intention of self-questioning, and such feeling would be strengthened with the level intonation — tone 3 in the definition of Halliday (1967a, 1970). Opposite to the examples in (13) above, this category is mainly construed as self-utterance; in other words, this class of utterances are not intended to talking to others as communicating something.

To conclude this section: the entire system of the Japanese PFPs would be

CHAPTER 5 THE INTERPERSONAL-NUANCE CARRIERS IN JAPANESE   83

enormous and need large amount of data and argumentation. As far as that which has been done in this section, however, it is clarified that the category of Japanese PFPs embodies rich varieties of the interpersonal nuances. The English equivalents of the nuances implied in Japanese are: exclamatory clauses, phonological prominence, tag questions and intonation.

In regard to the tripartite in (1) in Section 2, PFPs are to be classified in the lexicogrammar stratum, besides which phonology is also concerned in intonation, vowel length, prominence and so on. Still, however, PFPs basically belong to the level of lexicogrammar.

5.5 Modal Auxiliaries

Below is a tentative illustration of the Japanese Theme + Rheme structure, considering the interpersonal nuance carriers of case particles, modal auxiliaries and PFPs:

(15)

Theme		Rheme		
Subject	Case Particle	Predicate	Modal Aux.	PFP

kyou	wa	kayoubi	dat-ta	yo ne
today	TOPIC	Tuesday	PAST-DEC	PFP PFP

'It is Tuesday today, isn't it?'

It is evident from this table that many interpersonal elements are concerned with Theme + Rheme structure, which may entail a hypothesis that there would be some modification in the Japanese consideration within the SFL scheme.

As the label *modal* auxiliaries manifests *per se*, those predicates which belong to this category convey interpersonal meanings. The categories and meanings carried by modal auxiliaries would be of enormous diversity. From the viewpoint that modal auxiliaries are universal, it will be interesting to contrast among the various languages of the world.

Though the data are already old-fashioned to the eyes of the current speakers of Japanese, Tokieda (1978) analyzes colloquial Japanese and postulates the following semantic categories for auxiliary verbs:

(16) affirmative, negative, past/perfective, willingness/conjecture, honorific

The dispute below in this section will be challenging question, its wording typically depending on the interpersonal elements. The degree of politeness is mainly differentiated by the usage of auxiliaries in Japanese *da-desu-gozaimasu*:

84

(17) a. (Kimi wa)   dare   da.   'Who is it? / Who are you?'
         you   TOPIC who   DECLARATIVE   (the meaning is the same for b,c)
     b. (Anata wa) donata   desu   ka.
         you   who   DECLARATIVE   INTERROGATIVE
     c. Anata-sama   wa   dotira-sama de gozaimasu. ka.
         you-HONORIFIC   who   DECLARATIVE

Of these three questioning patterns, the first one (a) is uttered with falling into-nation and the other two with politer rising key.

The triad *da-desu-gozaimasu* is arranged in the order less to politer. Though these utterances in (17) vary in the degrees of politeness, the English translation can be expressed just as 'who is it/ who are you,' and can not reflecte the wording in Japanese. Of the choice 'who is it?' and 'who are you?' the former is neutral in terms of the interpersonal aspects, and consequently sounds politer than the latter. Questioning who the addressee is a face-threatening act *per se*.

In the three ways of the Japanese politeness difference in (17), not only auxiliaries but also the subjects must be distinguished. If the subject is *kimi* and the modal is *gozaimasu* in the same utterance, i.e. '*kimi-wa dare-de gozaimasu-ka*,' it sounds quite inconsistent and strange, because the subject is less polite while the predicate is the politest.

The most interesting finding of the three patterns (a-c) is that the speaker, the hearer and the relation between them are specified. The least polite version (a) can be typically spoken by a middle aged, man of socially status. The opposite (c), the politest one, is supposed to be addressed to the person in the senior position, since such formal attitude is required.

There are some other thought-provoking aspects in (17). The first point is that the alternation in the subject. As there are innumerable forms of pronouns—or, it may be appropriate to think of the category of pronouns as somewhat different from that in English—, several combinations of the subject and the predicate are possible. Further, ellipsis of part of predicate is another option, adding diversity to the speaker's choice. Below listed are some of such variations:

(18) a. Kimi-wa dare desu-ka.
     b. Anata-wa dare?
     c. Anata-wa donata desyou ka.

When comparing (17) and (18), as well as the similar situations of the choice of the second person pronoun, we can point out one inclination that *anata* may be used more frequently by female speakers. This kind of gender discrepancies are more conspicuous in Japanese than in English.

CHAPTER 5 THE INTERPERSONAL-NUANCE CARRIERS IN JAPANESE

The second point is subject ellipsis, indicated by the parentheses in (17), which will be less likely in the telephone conversations than in face-to-face exchange. Such omission of the subject itself is, however, informal, hence it would be inappropriate to omit in the polite predicate as in (c).

The last and a minor aspect is the attachment of a suffix -*sama* to *anata* in the politest version. In spite of the dichotomy between less polite *kimi* and politer *anata*, there are no inherent forms politer than *anata*, hence -*sama* is suffixed to make it suit for the predicate *gozaimasu*.

The honorific auxiliary system testified in this section is peculiar to Japanese, not found in English nor Chinese. In this regard the Japanese honorific system can be classified as lexicogrammar. So is the choice of pronoun forms, interrelated to modal auxliary / predicate.

The Japanese SFPs, though those listed below are only a few among them, denote the modal meanings such as interrogation, imperative, exclamation, consent and confirmation:

(19) ka, na, no, koto, zo, wa, yo, tomo, ne, sa

It is distinctive in Japanese SFPs that each item is far from homogeneous as regards to age, gender, and geographical origin of the speaker. Common with all of them are that they are colloquial and informal. The above entries are typical with the Tokyoite speakers; *zo, tomo* are almost exclusively belong to the utterance by the male speakers, while *no, wa* are those of the female counterparts.

Among the various modal meaning denoted by the SFPs, some are concerned with the syntactic and semantic structure — interrogative, imperative, prohibition —, and others with interpersonal nuances of exclamation, demanding consent, confirmation, attention-calling, and hesitation. In a system network, this dichotomy can be illustrated as below:

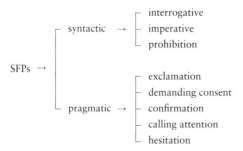

Figure 5.1: System network of SFPs

Of these categories, some such as the interrogative *ka* have been considered so far in relation to the clause intonation system. We will concentrate on the latter group in the rest of this section, as they would be parallel to English intonation and the Chinese particle systems.

The first category is the clauses of exclamation:

(20) a. kirei-da   naa
         beautiful   SFP   'How beautiful!'
     b. //ɪ ∧ it's / **very** / beautiful //

This type of the emotional announcement is akin to English clauses initiated with *How, What*. Another possible substitute in English is of a phonological nature as in (b): to emphasize with prominence falling on the modifier, in this case *very*. Semantically, such emphasis on the modifier is comparable to exclamatory clauses. The direct 'translation' of English *How beautiful!* into Japanese is *nante kirei (nan-darou)!*, which sounds too theatrical and showy, and is seldom to be uttered.

Next to be examined is demanding consent, and the resembling category of confirmation:

(21) a. atui   ne
         hot   SFP   'It's hot, isn't it?'
     b. kyou   wa   kayoubi   dat-ta   ne
         today TOPIC   Tuesday   COPULA-PAST   SFP
         'It's Tuesday today, isn't it?'

As the English translations manifest themselves, these categories of the demanding of consent and confirmation in Japanese are perfectly in agreement with tag questions in English. The most curious point with these categories is that the SFPs are obligatory in them. When speaking to another person / other people, they are ungrammatical without SFPs:

(21)′ a. *atui   b. *kyou-wa kayoubi dat-ta

These versions (21)′ are acceptable if they are spoken to the speaker himself/ herself. In this regard, the interpersonal aspect is mot important with these categories than in others — exclamation, attention-calling and hesitation — in which SFPs are optional.

The next examination is on the category of attention-calling:

(22) abunai   yo!
      dangerous   SFP   'Danger! / Watch out!'

CHAPTER 5   THE INTERPERSONAL-NUANCE CARRIERS IN JAPANESE   87

As a function of the clause, it needs no more explanation than the label *atten-tion-calling*. The possible situations suitable to this utterance will be of great diversity: a car is approaching to the hearer, or something is in front of the hearer while he/she walking and looking away from it, and so on. When any of the SFPs are attached, the utterance became tedious, as if any serious danger were far away.

The last consideration is on hesitation, or the self-questioning:

(23) dou   si-you   ka   na
     how   do-FUTURE   SFP   SFP   'What shall I do?'

The English translation is with the intention of self-questioning, and it will be strengthened with the level intonation — tone 3. Opposite to the examples in (21) above and not in (21)′, this category is mainly construed as self-utterance; in other words, this class of utterances are not intended to talking to others as communicating something.

To conclude this section: the entire system of the Japanese SFPs would be enormous and need large amount of data and argumentation. As far as that which has been done in this section, however, it is clarified the category of Japanese SFPs embodies rich varieties of the interpersonal nuances. The English equivalents of the nuances implied in Japanese are: exclamatory clauses, phonological prominence, tag questions and intonation. These correspondences will be diagrammed in section 8 below.

Though there are numbers of similarities between Japanese and Chinese SFPs, the direct comparison has not been made in this section. That will be one of the topics to be contrasted in the next section.

5.6 Semantics vs. Pragmatics: Conclusion

In this section, we will first summarize each category of the Japanese interpersonal nuance carriers in terms of the level of the semiotic system.

Intonation belongs to the domain of phonology, while it would be appropriate to classify final and case particles, modal auxiliaries belonging to lexicogrammar. Each of these four categories is concerned with interpersonal aspects. Of the three strata of discourse semantics, lexicogrammar and phonology / graphology, discourse semantics alone has not been applicable to any examples, since there have not been examples of larger than clauses.

Roughly speaking, however, discourse as a continuum of clauses SHOULD reflect interpersonal aspects such as human relationships of age, junior—senior order, kinship. These elements definitely affect wording in discourse. In

Japanese, for example, speaker must choose a polite style when addressing to senior members or speaking in public. What is called the 'silver' text (Halliday (1994, Appendix 1)) is an archetype of an organized chunk of a discourse in English, and in the analysis is overtly exemplified the relation between the speaker and the hearer. There, the speaker's intention to educate the hearer is reflected in, for instance, the address 'Anne.' The longer a discourse may be, the more pragmatic reflections should be considered.

As briefly mentioned in Section 1, it is PFPs in Japanese that is most important in carrying interpersonal nuances, and intonation key in English.

Up to this point, pragmatic perspective has not been reflected in the SFL framework. Apart from the question how to dub it within the Hallidayan outline, let us look at an integrated illustration of the semiotic and pragmatic systems. The revised version of the scheme of (1) in Section 1 is as follows, with the pragmatic sphere surrounded by the double line:

Table 5.1: SFL and pragmatics

This diagram suggests that each of discourse semantics in the narrow sense, lexico-grammar and phonology / graphology contains pragmatic elements, and the border between them are indicated by a wave line. In the level of phonology, intonation key carries interpersonal nuances. Particles and modal auxiliaries belong to the lexicogrammar stratum, conveying various semantic and pragmatic meanings.

As a conclusion, SFL does not have to establish *pragmatics* as one of the strata within the metafunction frameworks like the three levels in the semiotic system; instead, each of other means, such as Theme + Rheme, Mood + Residue, conveys interpersonal nuances.

Notes
1 It is needless to point out here that the subject is not explicit in Japanese; so it is possible to interpret this utterance as indicating 'Do you wear this one?' But the latter is less probable since to ask someone if he/she wants to wear something may sound somewhat strange.

CHAPTER 6

An Acoustic Analysis of the Punch Line Paratone in the *Kobanashi* Stories

6.1 Introduction

In this chapter, the examples of the punch line paratones will be analyzed based on the definitions given in the previous chapters. The target of the analysis in this chapter is the shorter *Kobanashi* stories.

The most significant difference of the types of the punch lines would be whether they are told by one of the characters or by the narration. In the English jokes, the variations of the style of the jokes seem to be more diverse than in the Japanese jokes. In the Japanese jokes, the dialogue style is unmarked while the narration or the monologue style is marked. The cause of the markedness of the punch lines told by the narration seems to be connected with the history of the Rakugo and the Kobanashi stories. The Rakugo hon-pen are the prolonged version of the shorter Kobanashi stories. Even in the Kobanashi stories, the basis of the discourse structure had been the dialogues between two characters. In the course of the development of the prolongation from the Kobanashi stories, the gesture were added: shifts right and left in order to distinguish between characters (*kamishimo*). With this gesture of kamishimo, it is inferred that the dialogue between two people is unmarked.

The Paratone is defined somewhat differently from one author to another. Brown and Yule (1983: 100), for example, describe it as follows:

> The "speech paragraph," or Paratone, like the orthographic paragraph, is identified by its boundary markers.... At the beginning of a paratone, the speaker typically uses an introductory expression to announce what he specifically intends to talk about. This introductory expression is made phonologically prominent and the whole of the first clause or sentence in a Paratone may be uttered with raised pitch. The end of a Paratone ... can be marked by very low pitch, loss of amplitude, and a lengthy pause.

Tench (1996: 24) develops these observations of the low pitch, the loss of amplitude and a lengthy pause, and presents the phonetic and phonological description of the Paratone in more detail, as shown in the previous chapter.

In the following sections, several Kobanashi stories will be analyzed acoustically. My hypothesis is that the punch line paratones are not always necessary in the Kobanashi stories, mainly because they are short. Contrastively, the longer hon-pen stories need punch line paratone, mainly because punch line paratone signals the end of the story. The results of the Kobanashi stories below would endorse this hypothesis.

6.2 Japanese *Kobanashi*

The history of Japanese traditional funny stories *Kobanashi* (literally 'small story') is closely related with that of *Rakugo*. The ultimate origin of Rakugo goes back to some 400 years ago when story-tellers entertained their samurai feudal lords. About 60 years after that — around 1680 — in Kyoto and Osaka, Rakugo originated in public spaces such as in shrines and temples, while in Edo it was performed in tatami rooms. In those days, there used to be only shorter anecdotes that lasted for a few minutes. About 300 years ago, the format of *Rakugo* resembled that of the current style. The stories had become longer and longer, with improvements added one after another. The longest ones take more than one hour nowadays.

When reviewing the history of *Rakugo*, it is assumed that shorter stories, i.e. 'ko-banashi,' have developed into longer ones. The longer stories will be defined as 'hon-pen' (literally *main stories*) tentatively here. It is often the case that some short stories are told before the longer main story. Such short stories are called *makura* in Japanese, literally *a pillow*, because a pillow is put under the head (hon-pen).

There are six stories told as Makura before the main *Rakugo* 'Goko'(literally: 'five lights') performed by Master Katsura Beichou (available on Youtube). The main story 'Goko' is a kind of a ghost story, and hence the following six Kobanashis deal with ghosts, monsters, goblins and so on. The order of the six stories told in the performance are:

(1)   1. Abura-ya (Oil Merchant)
     2. Kamo to negi (A Duck and Scallion)
     3. Kaita mon ga mono iuta (Written Documents are Eloquent)
     4. Bakemon o nega-e (Suitable for a Spook)
     5. Yuurei no ana (A Haunted Hole)
     6. Bakemon no enkai (Monsters' Party)

CHAPTER 6 AN ACOUSTIC ANALYSIS OF THE PUNCH LINE PARATONE IN THE *KOBANASHI* STORIES   91

Among these six, the shortest two — *Kamo to negi* and *Aburaya* — will be presented with the pitch charts so that the intonation patterns are visible. The third one, i.e. *Kaita mon ga mono iuta*, will be presented with the original Japanese and the English word-for-word translation without the pitch charts because it is too long. The order of the acoustic analyses is arranged from the shorter ones to the longer ones.

6.2.1 *Kamo to Negi*

The first to be analyzed is the shortest one *Kamo to Negi* (A Duck and Scallion):

(2) Episode 1: Duck and Scallion (*Kamo to Negi*)
  1. Kamo ga   koo kawa oyoide-tan-desu   naa
     duck   NOM thus river swim-PAST-POLITE   PART(icle)
  2. hona kamo no oyoi-deru   ushiro-kara   negi ga koo nagarete-kite
     then   GEN   PROG   back-from   scallion   flow-come
  3. ushiro e   poon-to   atat-ta
             toward suddenly-QUOT   hit-PAST
  4. Kamo ga   hyot-to   furimui-te,
               swiftly   turn
  5. "Oo, kowa…"
     oh horrible
  Narration: When a duck is swimming in the river, a piece of scallion flows from the upper stream and strikes the duck. The duck said, "How horrible…"

This story is based on the popular Japanese idiom "kamo ga negi shotte yatte-kuru" – literally 'a duck comes along with a scallion on its back.' The funniness of this story will need a background explanation; in traditional Japanese cuisine, duck is an ideal ingredient, and a scallion is also suitable as a side ingredient, especially when they are cooked together in one pot. Hence, it is a premise that a duck that comes along with a scallion is the most favorable situation for a human being to eat the *kamo-nabe* (duck pot). Under this premise, ducks MUST be afraid of the situation in which they are with a scallion. Hence when a duck happens to come upon a scallion, it would be an ultimate occasion to be afraid of.

The pitch contour charts of these five lines are as follows:

(3)

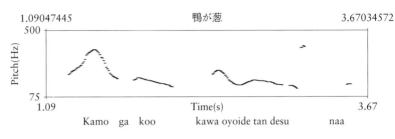

Kamo ga koo   kawa oyoide tan desu   naa

(4)

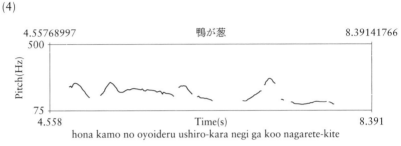

hona kamo no oyoideru ushiro-kara negi ga koo nagarete-kite

(5)

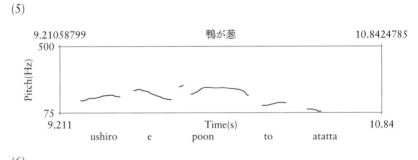

ushiro   e   poon   to   atatta

(6)

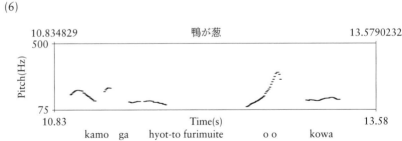

kamo ga   hyot-to furimuite   o o   kowa

Being different from the transcription in English in Kadooka (2012a), the tonic syllables are not so significant in Japanese phonology. Hence, the designation for the tonic syllables will not be explicit in the transcriptions.

Here is a table showing the average, min(imum), max(imum) frequencies and the range between the minimum and the maximum, duration of each line in

CHAPTER 6 AN ACOUSTIC ANALYSIS OF THE PUNCH LINE PARATONE IN THE *KOBANASHI* STORIES   93

seconds, the number of morae (μ)[1], the tempo (duration divided by the number of the morae) and the pause before each line. The lowest in average, minimum, and maximum, the narrowest in range, the slowest tempo, and the longest pause are indicated in bold type[2]:

Table 6.1: Pitch transitions in *Kamo to negi*

	ave.	min.	max.	range	D	μ	Tempo	Pause
1	211.52	127.01	400.31	273.30	2.45	11	0.22	
2	185.52	113.59	281.12	167.53	3.87	26	0.15	1.10
3	184.12	**82.42**	248.60	166.18	1.50	12	0.13	**1.30**
4	**151.19**	97.91	**215.89**	**117.98**	0.85	11	**0.08**	0.35
5	161.13	83.46	314.79	231.33	0.83	4	0.21	0.62
ave	178.70	100.88	292.14	191.26	1.90	12.8	0.16	0.84

The most peculiar point in this episode from the narrative perspective is that there is only one character: the duck. In addition, the only utterance by the character terminates the story, i.e. the punch line "Oo, kowa..." From the hearing impression, this mutter is emotional, especially with the interjection "Oo." This emotional expression is reflected in the widest range among the five lines. Another interesting movement of the pitch contour is the very beginning of the episode, "Kamo ga ...": here realizes the highest pitch in the whole episode of 400.31 Hz. This suits the observation in (2) of the high in the beginning. Compared with those of a British speaker's voice in Kadooka (2011b)[3], Master Beichou's voice is much higher. It is specific that the maximum pitches are relatively higher than the British speaker when compared with the average and the minimum pitches.

In the pre-punch line, the average and maximum frequencies are the lowest, and the range is the narrowest: the fourth line. The narrowest range means that the utterance is monotonous because the difference between the highest and the lowest tone of voice is the smallest. The lowest minimum pitch is observed in line 3. When we contrast those of the punch line with the average of the five lines, the average and the minimum are lower, though the maximum is higher and the range is wider. The tempo is slower than the average. Generally speaking, the observations in (2) are appropriate in table 6.1.

Next is the change of the maximum, average and minimum frequencies through the episode.

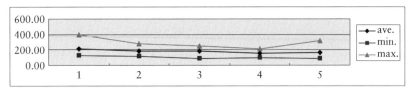

Figure 6.1: Pitch transitions in *Kamo to negi*

The 'gradual lowering' in (2) is best observed with the baseline, or the low pitches, rather than the highest and the average counterparts. In this illustration, the appropriateness of the gradual lowering is applied to the low pitches, not the high or the average.

6.2.2 *Abura-ya no Neko*

The second episode is more than three times longer than the first one, lasting for about 41 seconds. Below are the transcription and the intonation charts:

(7) Episode 2 : Oil Merchant (*Abura-ya*)
   1. Abura-ya no yane ni yo na yo na bake-neko ga deru to-iu uwasa ga tat-te...
   2. Kinjo no renchuu ga sore o iron-na koto ii-masu node abura-ya no shujin ga ki-ni-shimashi-te yonaka ni
   3. oki-dashite jibun-toko no yane o mi-masu to iu to ma-yonaka ni oo-yane no teppen-e
   4. sugoi kono neko ga
   5. gira-gira —to me o hikarashi-nagara oni-gawara ni koo te   o kake-te
   6. gya - to nai-teru
   7. "Koitsu kai,
   8. kora, omae-no okage de obake-abura ya to ka iron-na koto i-ware-n ne ya.
   9. Nande uchi ni de-yaga-n ne ya, kono neko."
   10. Ishi o tsukande abura-ya no shujin ga pa—t to nage-tsukeru to, neko ga hyot-to tai kawashi-te,
   11. "Abura-ya no."

Narration: Once, there was a rumor that a ghost cat haunted the roof of an oil merchant's store. The master of the store made up his mind to probe whether the rumor was true or false. At midnight, when he was patrolling, he found the cat and said:

Master: Owing to you, our oil is dubbed as haunted, and we have a lot of trouble.

Narration: Then the master threw a stone at the cat. The cat dodged it and

said:
Cat: Dangerous!

(8)

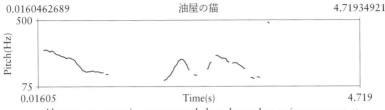

Abura-ya no yane ni   yo na yo na bake-neko ga deru to iu uwasa ga tatte

(9)

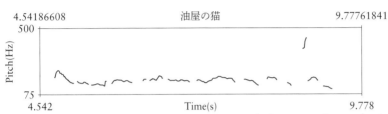

kinjo no renchuu ga sore o iron-na koto iimasu node abura-ya no shujin ga ki ni shimashi te yonaka ni

(10)

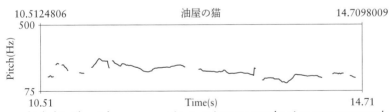

oki-dashite jibun-toko no yane o mimasu to iu to ma-yonaka ni oo-yane no teppen he

(11)

(12)

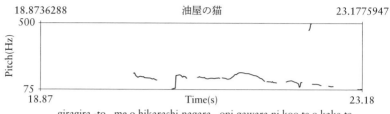

giragira -to   me o hikarashi-nagara   oni-gawara ni koo te o kake-te

(13)

gya -- to naiteru

(14)

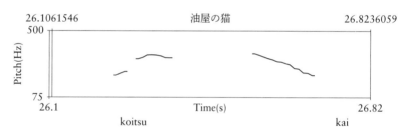

koitsu   kai

(15)

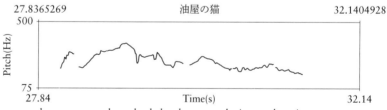

kora omae-no okage de obake-abura ya to ka iron-na koto iware n ne ya

(16)

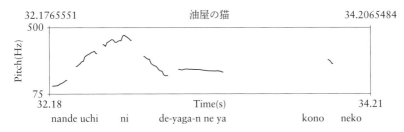

(17)

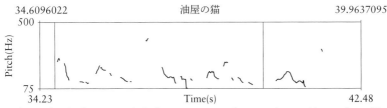

(18)

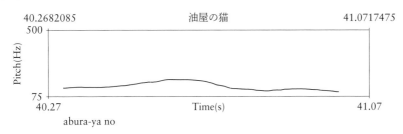

The punch line is a pun of "abuna-ya-no" ('dangerous' followed by particles 'ya' and 'no') and "abura-ya-no" (oil merchant). In the actual performance by Master Beichou, the oil-merchant master's tone of voice is a little louder than usual, reflecting his excitement. Then the punch line by the cat in line 11 is suddenly lowered, disappointing the listener's expectation that follows the former master's appeal to the cat. If this punch line were to be uttered similarly to the former excited tone, it would sound highly out of place.

From the perspective of the discourse structure, this is a 'dialogue' between an oil merchant master and a cat. The master speaks to the cat complaining about its appearance on the roof of the shop, and the cat 'replies' after the throwing of a stone.

From the lexical perspective, some onomatopoeic expressions are phonologically prominent in this episode: *gira-gira* in line 5 depicting the manner of dazzling of the cat's eyes; *gyaa* in line 6, the coercive sound of the cat on the roof; *paa* in line 10, the manner of the oil-merchant's master throwing a stone, and *hyoQ* in line 10, the manner of the cat's dodging the stone. These words are prosodically prominent in that the higher pitch and/or the stronger amplitude and/or the slower tempo are combined. In the above charts (11) through (18), however, neither the pitch nor the amplitude is visible.[4] Only the cat's sound *gyaa* in line 6 is verifiable in the chart. The sound 'gyaaa...' lasts for 1.54 seconds (one syllable) while 'to nai-teru' (four syllables and five morae) for 0.62 second. If counted simply, the duration of the sound 'gyaa...' is about 2.48 times of 'to nai-teru,' hence it would be about fifteen morae. But from the practical account, it is not proper to assign fifteen morae to the sole syllable 'gyaa....' Tentatively, five morae are assigned for this phrase.

Below is the table of the average, minimum, maximum frequencies, the range, duration, the number of the morae, the tempo and the pause before each line:

Table 6.2: Pitch transitions in *Aburaya*

	ave.	min.	max.	range	D	µ	Tempo	pause
1	219.00	114.30	312.03	197.73	4.04	29	0.14	
2	168.59	108.68	221.91	113.23	5.24	38	0.14	0.44
3	202.81	126.59	285.70	159.11	4.20	36	0.12	1.27
4	162.23	85.53	252.36	166.83	1.90	8	0.24	1.51
5	146.77	76.84	183.58	106.74	4.30	27	0.16	0.74
6	148.94	124.31	163.72	39.41	2.16	10	0.22	0.26
7	297.52	216.12	354.99	138.87	0.72	5	0.14	0.74
8	248.72	166.64	364.45	197.81	3.48	31	0.11	1.34
9	275.64	126.12	449.66	323.54	2.03	16	0.13	0.56
10	164.68	77.96	270.46	192.50	5.33	33	0.16	0.48
11	137.76	86.02	183.85	97.83	0.80	5	0.16	0.30
ave	197.51	119.01	276.61	157.60	3.11	21.6	0.16	0.76

Compared with the shorter episode *Kamo Negi*, this one consists of eleven intonational units, and the duration is more than three times as long. Consequently, the results of the highlighted cells scatter in various lines. The slowest tempo is in line 4, the lowest minimum and the maximum frequencies in line 5, the narrowest range in line 6, and the lowest average frequency in the punch line. In addition, we find lengthy lines consisting of more than 30 morae, whereas three shorter lines —i.e. 4, 7 and 11— are less than 10 morae. The mean number of morae is 21.6 overall.

It is interesting that both the lowest minimum and the maximum pitches are realized in the same line: the fifth line. This line is a long one — longer than the average of 21.6 morae per line —, consisting of 27 morae. The lowest average pitch is, on the other hand, in the punch line, and the baseline is the second lowest with the difference of 0.49 Hz. That is to say, the punch line is near to the lowest in the whole story. The pause before the punch line is, however, 0.3 second and is much shorter than the average pause of 0.76 second.

The transitions of the maximum, average and the minimum pitches are as follows:

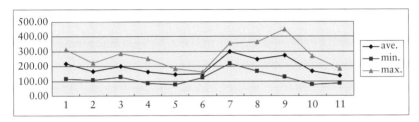

Figure 6.2: Pitch transition in *Aburaya*

The transition of the baseline frequencies is not so straightforward as in (11) for Episode 2. We can observe a general lowering from line 1 toward line 5, but then there is rising to lines 6 and 7. From line 7, there is again a lowering process toward the end of the story. Such a bumpy movement of the baseline may come from the thrilling development of the story when a monstrous cat appears on the roof of an oil merchant, and then comes the master of the merchant, bringing in a skirmish between the two. If we consider the peak of the strain is expressed by the highest maximum pitch, it is in line 9. The next line — the tenth line — is the pre-punch line, and hence the tone is suddenly lowered, especially in the latter half 'neko ga hyot-to tai kawashi-te (the cat nimbly dodged the body).

6.2.3 *Kaita Mon ga Mono Iuta*

The next one *Kaita-mon ga Mono Iuta* (Written Documents are Eloquent) is the longest of the three, consisting of 48 intonational units and lasting for two minutes and eight seconds.

(19)
1. Yonaka   ni ne,
   midnight at PART

2. benjo ni iku kuse ga   tsuku, are kuse ni naru   mon-desu   na
   toilet to go habit NOM attach   that   become   thing-POLITE PART

3. Decchi-san ga   kanarazu ma-yonaka ni
   apprentice-TITLE surely

4. toire iki-tou naru-n desu na, you o   tashi-tou naru.
   toilet go-want become errand   ACC   run-want

5. Nemutai me kosuri-nagara,   daitai sono, mukashi no decchi nante mono wa,
   sleepy eye rub-as   generally well years-ago   as-for thing
   ne-tara, doro no you ni, shin-da you ni nemuru mon desu   ga,
   sleep-get mud   like   deadly   thing POLITE though
   kuse no mono wa shaa-nai, yonaka ni moyooshi-te kuru.
                   no use   feel-like   come

6. Ban no toire cchuu no wa, mukashi no benjo wa, kowakat-ta desu na.
   night GEN   QUOT   TOPIC   horrible-PAST

7. Soko e   kou...
   There toward thus

8. it-te gaman-shiteru to,   yappari kou furui hito ga majinai o oshie-te kureru
   go patience-do then also   old   person spell   teach BENEFICIAL

9. (Bantou)   "Omae naa,   kon-ya yo-naka benjo e i-tara na,
   (adult clerk)   you   PART   tonight

10. mukou it-te, shita o   mui-te
    there go   below toward turn

11. 'Myouban   kara you sanji-mahen,'   to konai ie.
    tomorrow-night from   can't come-not   thus say (imperative)

12. Honna,   ashita kara ko-n   you ni naru   sakai.
    then   tomorrow come-NEG like   become because

13. Sou iu, majinai ga an-ne ya."
    such   exist

14. (Decchi)   "Sayo ka..."
    (Apprentice) I see...

15. Decchi mo   issho-kenmei des-sakai,
    TOPIC   with-strength POLITE

16. yonaka ni nemutai me kosuri-nagara toire ite, you tashi-ta ato, shita no
    sleepy   eye rub-PROG
    hou mui-te,
    direction

17. (Decchi) "Myouban kara you sanji-mahen."

18. (Mono no ke) "Sou iw-an to mata oi-de."
    (Strange voice) so say-never again come-IMPERATIVE

19. (Decchi) "Kyaaa!" (screaming)

CHAPTER 6 AN ACOUSTIC ANALYSIS OF THE PUNCH LINE PARATONE IN THE *KOBANASHI* STORIES   101

20. Ki-ushinau   no   atarimae desu wa, kora.
    lose-consciousness COPULA logical   PART   this

21. Oo-sawagi ni   nat-te ne,
    uproar   RESULT become-PAST

22. (Bantou)   "Donai shi-ta?"
    (adult clerk) how   do-PAST

23. (Decchi)   "Iya, shita kara   koe ga kikoe-ta."
    (Apprentice) well   voice hear-PAST

24. (Bantou)   "Sonna aho na koto   ga aru kai,
    (adult clerk) such   silly thing   PART

25. sora omae ga   ne-toboke-ten ne ya."
    that   half-asleep

26. (Decchi) "Sonna koto nai."
              No way.

27. Tsugi no hi, mata kowa-gowa i-te,
    next day   again timidly   go

28. (Decchi)   "Myouban kara you sanji-mahen."

29. (Mono no ke)   "Sou iw-an to mata oide."

30. Kondo wa bantou ya   nanka ga kii-te   tan-de,
    this-time clerk   TOPIC like   hear-PAST because

31. (Bantou)   "Korya, erai   koccha,
    (adult clerk) this   serious   thing

32. uchi-no benjo ni nani-ka koo, kaii ga   okot-ta,"   cchuu wake de,
    our   something mystery happen   reason

33. dee, iroiro to go-kitou ya   toka, majinai ya toka, mou, nanja, bon-san ni
    then various prayer TOPIC and   Buddhist-monk
    nan-ka o-kyou agete moro-tari shite mo, kore ga yami-mahen no ya naa.
    some   sutra   receive   cease-NOT

34. Kanarazu   henji shi-yoru.
    necessarily reply do-DEROGATORY

35. Shinrui ni hitori   gurai, sono, nan-demo you shit-te-ru cchuna ossan
    relatives one-person about well anything well know   man
    chuna ori-man nen, kore.
    like   exist

36. Doko no shinrui demo, mukashi wa ot-tan da,   kou-iu benri-na   hito ga na,
    any   even   exist-PAST such   convenient person

37. "Washi ga mite-yarou," cchuu wake de yat-te kite, benjo no naka,
    I   look-give   come come-PAST inside
    "Nani   mo   ayashii mono nasa-   sou ya nai-kai, uhm..."
    nothing TOPIC strange   NOT-exist like

38. Yoko o miru-to,
    side look
39. tsumari   toiretto-peepaa desu na, ima de iyaa,,,[5]
    that-is-to-say toilet-paper   now   say
40. otoshi-gami,,,
    (toilet paper)
41. sore ga shoumon no furui non ya   toka,
    they   contract   old ones TOPIC and
42. choubo-rui no furu-nat-ta   yatsu o kou,
    account books old-become-PAST ones
43. tekitou-na   ookisa ni kit-te, tsun-de aru.
    approapriate size   cut   lay-in-heaps
44. (Mono-shiri) "Kora, nan ya"
                        what
45. (Bantou) "Kora, shoumon ya choubo no furui yatsu o otoshi-gami ni
    tsuko-te man-nen."
    These are old account books and notes for toilet paper.
46. (Mono-shiri) "Kore ga ika-n."
                        no-good
47. (Bantou)   "Sayo ka."
    (Is that so?)
48. (Mono-shiri)   "Kaita mon ga mono iu-ta."
                     written   things say-PAST

A child apprentice, who is in his early teens, has trouble with his habit of
waking up and going to the toilet at midnight while he is asleep. One day an
adult clerk said, "Well, I will show you a good spell. When you finish, look
below and say "I won't come tomorrow night." Then you won't have to go
to the toilet any more." The apprentice thanked and when he went to the toilet that night, he said "I won't come tomorrow night." A strange voice,
"Don't say such a thing and come again."replied from below, and the apprentice lost consciousness. The next night, the colleague clerks went with
the apprentice, and the same strange voice replied. They all wondered why
such a strange voice replied, and asked the Buddhist monks to pray for the
stopping of such a mystery, but the replies never ceased. Then came a knowledgeable person to the merchant, saying "I can solve the problem." He
looked around in the toilet, and asked about the toilet paper. "What are
these?" "Well, they are written documents and account books which are cut
into small pieces" "They are the cause of the trouble." "Why?" "Written
documents said something / Written documents are eloquent."

The main character is the child apprentice (lines 14, 17, 19, 23, 26 and 28) who

CHAPTER 6 AN ACOUSTIC ANALYSIS OF THE PUNCH LINE PARATONE IN THE *KOBANASHI* STORIES   103

seems to be in his early teens, and the supporting part played by the adult clerk (lines 8, 9, 10, 11, 12, 13, 22, 24, 25, 31, 32, 45 and 47). This shows that the clerk keeps the most numerous speaking turns. The most important role in the sense that he tells the punch line of the whole story, is a knowledgeable man (lines 37, 44, 46 and 48). Not explicit in the remarks, there would be other apprentices and clerks working with the merchant. Another important *character*, but not actually seen, is a strange voice (lines 18 and 29), speaking the same content ("Sou iw-an to, mata oi-de.": *Never say such a thing, and come again.*). Hence, this is not a dialogue but a group play. The speaker-to-speaker acoustic analyses will be given after the presentation of the whole table.

The core of the discourse is the repetition of the apprentice's "Myouban kara you sanji-mahen" (From tomorrow night on, I can not come (here to the toilet)) and the reply by the strange voice "Sou iw-an to, mata oide" (Never say such a thing, and please come again). When we include the adult clerk's teaching, "Myouban kara you sanji-mahen" is repeated three times. During the repetition, the listeners would wonder how the story would progress, and what the ending would be like. Then comes the punch line that 'the written documents are eloquent.' Though corresponding proverbs to the lesson of this punch line are not found in English, the same idea would be easily understandable in contract-dominant societies.

Here is a table presenting the main data of 48 lines:

Table 6.3: Pitch transitions of Episode 3

	ave.	min.	max.	range	D	μ	tempo	pause
1	179.04	89.28	285.57	196.29	0.81	5	0.16	
2	193.85	121.22	383.23	262.01	2.14	23	0.09	0.78
3	237.76	166.34	392.53	226.19	2.34	15	0.16	0.74
4	125.64	77.18	186.62	109.44	2.29	22	0.10	0.74
5	210.71	97.96	416.49	318.53	8.28	74	0.11	0.21
6	167.64	105.75	329.46	223.71	3.03	27	0.11	1.56
7	131.35	82.99	293.92	210.93	0.74	5	0.15	0.85
8	172.06	76.53	397.39	320.86	4.56	34	0.13	1.16
9	133.11	103.15	177.97	74.82	2.79	19	0.15	0.51
10	138.16	100.19	153.97	53.78	1.34	13	0.10	0.96
11	182.48	79.73	262.43	182.70	2.41	20	0.12	0.17
12	116.44	77.03	138.31	61.28	1.63	18	0.09	0.95
13	123.08	80.56	133.83	53.27	1.21	13	0.09	0.25
14	132.03	125.97	139.60	13.63	0.68	3	0.23	0.36

15	115.07	77.57	151.77	74.20	1.26	17	0.07	0.36
16	119.35	93.70	152.97	59.27	2.93	36	0.08	1.01
17	234.73	186.90	291.53	104.63	1.91	14	0.14	0.82
18	175.85	135.75	221.04	85.29	1.20	11	0.11	0.28
19	440.50	380.65	474.13	93.48	0.58	4	0.15	0.40
20	223.23	131.32	301.59	170.27	1.68	18	0.09	2.93
21	397.59	221.57	422.45	200.88	1.21	10	0.12	1.26
22	251.87	144.24	372.83	228.59	0.44	5	0.09	0.54
23	198.18	140.88	296.14	155.26	1.38	13	0.11	0.00
24	199.24	77.42	310.95	233.53	1.32	13	0.10	0.00
25	223.69	168.38	349.68	181.30	1.25	14	0.09	0.37
26	246.68	121.87	336.30	214.43	0.72	7	0.10	0.56
27	142.59	98.13	241.90	143.77	1.55	12	0.13	0.50
28	125.03	77.33	193.98	116.65	1.56	14	0.11	0.39
29	236.35	169.70	277.43	107.73	1.38	11	0.13	0.20
30	153.85	89.30	236.66	147.36	2.06	19	0.11	0.60
31	259.41	142.43	334.01	191.58	1.14	8	0.14	0.66
32	153.23	76.08	266.22	413.60	3.93	26	0.15	1.44
33	161.72	68.53	258.84	190.31	8.02	59	0.14	0.47
34	181.90	96.28	266.15	169.87	1.12	10	0.11	0.54
35	206.31	75.01	345.63	270.62	3.79	40	0.09	1.72
36	169.76	91.55	211.67	120.12	2.81	30	0.09	0.27
37	155.92	75.21	250.66	175.45	5.30	45	0.12	0.26
38	227.74	122.82	295.39	172.57	0.79	6	0.13	0.78
39	127.88	85.28	241.47	156.19	1.88	21	0.09	0.45
40	163.23	99.97	213.88	113.91	0.56	5	0.11	0.31
41	201.22	96.41	317.03	220.62	2.24	16	0.14	0.61
42	175.26	106.94	233.12	126.18	1.81	16	0.11	0.11
43	163.53	83.87	210.65	126.78	1.68	18	0.09	0.26
44	222.00	163.72	309.24	145.52	0.42	5	0.08	0.07
45	161.86	102.62	230.68	128.06	2.80	30	0.09	0.72
46	270.80	229.19	307.50	78.31	0.78	6	0.13	1.69
47	65.07	63.79	65.73	1.94	0.47	3	0.16	0.40
48	160.92	78.24	231.52	153.28	1.46	11	0.13	0.46
ave	186.56	115.76	269.00	153.24	2.04	18.0	0.12	0.65

As the whole episode is lengthy, the duration of each line varies one after another. While the short lines are less than ten morae, the longest line consists of 74 morae, lasting for 8.28 seconds (line 5). The mean tempo per mora is 0.12 second, which is faster than those of 0.16 in the first two episodes.

The extremity of the low pitches concentrate in the pre-punch line (line 47): the average, the minimum and the maximum.[6] Line 47 is a three-mora response "Sayo ka..." (Is that so?) by the clerk, sounding serious and solemn. The oppressed tone of voice multiplies the story-telling effect in the punch line; that is to say, the listeners are wondering how the whole episode terminates. Then the punch line releases the tension.

The second lowest baseline is in line 33, which is a long line lasting for 8.02 seconds. It is the narration, not a remark by the character. The second highest maximum appears in line 32, just before the lowest baseline; a remark by the adult clerk. This high pitch reflects the clerk's excitement and the anxiousness about the mystery. The longest pause is the one before line 20. The slowest tempo is realized in line 14, a reply "Sayo ka..." (I see...) by the apprentice.

The maximum in the first line 285.57 Hz is higher than the average 269.00 Hz. The baseline in the punch line 78.24 Hz is lower than the average 115.76 Hz. The pause before the punch line is 0.46 second, shorter than the average 0.65 second. The tempo of the punch line is 0.13 second per mora, longer than the average of 0.12 second per mora. Thus, as for this particular story, the observations for the punch line Paratone in (2) are appropriate except the longer pause.

This story is interesting when we analyze the acoustic figures with the distinctions of the speakers. The results are as follows:

Table 6.4: Table of the pitches by the characters

	ave.	min.	max.	range	D	μ	tempo	pause
clerk	167.67	99.40	245.69	146.30	1.95	16.62	0.12	0.63
apprentice	229.53	172.27	288.61	116.35	1.14	9.17	0.14	0.42
strange	206.10	152.73	249.24	96.51	1.29	11.00	0.12	0.24
knowledgeable	201.10	141.46	261.18	119.72	1.46	12.26	0.12	0.43

As expected, the child apprentice's voice is the highest while the adult clerk's is the lowest of all of the average, the maximum and the minimum. The range of the strange voice is the narrowest, and hence it is endorsed so that the voice sounds suppressed. The child's speeches (0.14 second per mora) are the fastest and the others are similar (0.12).

Though the whole story is a long one, the progress of the narration can be partly comprehensible with the transition of the pitches.

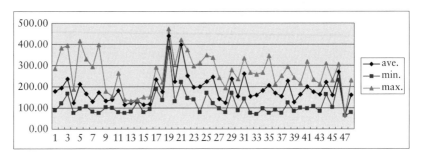

Figure 6.3: Transition of pitch in *Kaita mon ga mono iuta*

The most conspicuous trend through all the processes is the succession of the low tone in lines 12 to 16. In these five lines, the maximum pitches are 130 — 150 Hz, half of the average 280.82 Hz. Not only the maximum but also the average and the baseline are lower in these five lines. Lines 12 and 13 are the concluding part of the adult clerk's remark, line 14 is the reply by the apprentice, and lines 15 and 16 are narration. Such a succession of low tone of voice can be regarded as preparation for the sudden development of the story into a turmoil.

The next noticeable trend is the trough in line 47, which has already been pointed out above. This trough seems all the deeper because of the higher baseline in line 46, the remark by the knowledgeable man "Kore ga ikan" (This is no good). The higher pitches in line 46 are also in good contrast with the oppressed tone of voice in the punch line.

During the first one third of the story — until line 18 —, the average and the baseline pitches keep low, though the maximum shows some ups and downs. Then comes the scream by the apprentice in line 19, raising the maximum, average and the baseline altogether. Both the average and the baseline pitches are the highest here.

The first peak of the tension appears with the scream of the apprentice in line 19. The reason for the high pitches in this line may partly ascribed to the premise that this apprentice is a boy in his early teens, and hence the performer must raise his voice above his natural pitch. This manner of mimicking a boy's voice occurs in line 17 (average 234.73 Hz, minimum 186.90 Hz, maximum 291.53 Hz), but not so explicitly in the repetition of "Myouban kara you sanji-mahen" in line 28 (average 125.03 Hz, minimum 77.33 Hz, maximum 193.98 Hz). The low tone in line 28 may be nearer to Master Beichou's natural voice.

Thus, it can be hypothesized through the brief examinations of these three episodes that the ranges of tone of voice reflect the varieties of characters in each story. The simple structure is represented by *A Duck and Scallion*, in

CHAPTER 6 AN ACOUSTIC ANALYSIS OF THE PUNCH LINE PARATONE IN THE *KOBANASHI* STORIES 107

which only one character appears; the opposite case is *Written Documents are Eloquent*, in which at least four characters utter. Another possible factor that can affect the ranges of the pitch is the age and / or the gender of the character; that is to say, the pitches of children and women are higher than those of adult men. Considering that most of the characters in the Rakugo and Kobanashi stories are adult male, the ranges will be wider when women and/or children characters utter during the turns.

6.3 Conclusion

The last section was the acoustic examination of the six observations for the Paratone in (2). As shown there, most of the results such as High in the beginning, Slow in the punch line are consistent with the phonetic 'predictions' (2). The exceptions can be ascribed to the intended effect by the story-teller. In *Written Documents are Eloquent*, for example, the pre-punch line is the lowest tone and the baseline is raised in the punch line. This may be because the punch line "Kaita mon ga mono iu-ta" (*Written document said something.*) is a bit lengthy. In *A Duck and Scallion*, the baseline (83.46 Hz) is close to the lowest (82.42 Hz) and lowered from the pre-punch line. In *Oil Merchant*, the baseline in the punch line (86.02 Hz) is raised from the pre-punch line (77.96 Hz).

Let us summarize Tench (1996)'s definitions of the Paratone with three episodes in this chapter. Below are the definitions of the criteria (2) to analyze the phonetic data in the last section:

(20)　1. High in the beginning: The pitch of the onset syllable of the initial intonation unit is higher than the average of the whole intonation units.
　　　2. High baseline: The low pitches of the initial unit are relatively high, compared to the low pitches in the final unit of the paragraph.
　　　3. Gradual lowering: There is a gradual lowering of the baseline through the paragraph until the final unit.
　　　4. Slower tempo in the final: The duration per mora in the final unit is longer than the average of the whole paragraph.
　　　5. Longer pause before the final: The pause before the punch line is longer than the average of the whole paragraph.

Those cells that suit these criteria are with checks in the following table:

Table 6.5: Elements of punch line paratone

	Duck and scallion	Oil merchant	Written documents
High in the beginning	✓	✓	✓
High baseline	✓		
Gradual lowering	✓		
Slow in the punch line	✓		✓
Pause before the punch line	✓		

The *Duck and Scallion* episode perfectly satisfies the five definitions in (25). This can be ascribed to the peculiarity of this story in its length and that the duck is the only character and it utters "*Oo, kowa* .... (How horrible)." Before this punch line, there is a narration describing the situation. Such monologue style necessarily invites a monotonous manner of story-telling. In this particular case in *Duck and Scallion*, however, the story itself is so short that the listener will not think of the length of the story. The relationship between the length of the story and the number of the characters is endorsed by the facts that in the other two longer episodes — *Oil Merchant* and *Written Documents are Eloquent* --, there are more than two characters. That is to say, in order to distinguish several characters, the performer must vary the tones of voices, typically pitches. Apart from the numbers of characters in a story, higher pitches than his normal tone of voice are indispensable for an adult male teller when he pretends to be a child and/or a woman.

Gradual lowering is only one of the patterns of the transition of the baseline frequencies; if the story teller heightens the tone of voice to perform a child or a woman in the midst of the story, the gradual lowering pattern is not maintained. This is exemplified by the child clerk in *Written Documents are Eloquent*.

It is reasonable in the sense that the High in the beginning is functionally the realization of the High Paratone, which is consistent with the prediction. In the series of *Kobanashi* stories as the *Makura* of a Rakugo hon-pen, the first line of a new story must be signalled by the high tone of voice. Hence the High in the beginning is realized with all of the three stories.

Next to the High in the beginning is the Slow in the punch line; it is observed in *Duck and Scallion* and *Written Documents are Eloquent*. The duration per mora in the punch lines is longer than the average in these two. In the punch line of *Oil Merchant*, the duration per mora is 0.16 second, which is around the average. Hence it can be considered to be almost consistent with the Slow in the punch line criterion.

The others — High baseline, Gradual lowering and Pause before the punch line— are observed only in *Duck and Scallion*. As for the Pause before the punch line, for example, a lengthy pre-punch line is followed by the one-phrase punch line, and the pause between these two lines is only 0.30 second in *Oil Merchant*.

As only three stories have been analyzed in this chapter, the generalizations must be limited. Further examinations of tens or scores of stories are necessary to endorse the hypotheses (20).

Notes

1 A 'mora' is an idiosyncratic phonological / phonetic unit in Japanese. Morae reflect the units of the duration better than syllables. When measuring the duration of a moraic consonant (Q), a moraic nasal (N) or the prolongation of a vowel (R), they are regarded as equal to other independent syllables. This is the case when counting Haiku poetry as 5-7-5 and Tanka as 5-7-5-7-7.

2 The same is true for the tables of other stories.

3 The average frequency of the four English jokes told by a British speaker is around 130 Hz, the lowest is 80 Hz, the highest 170 Hz.

4 It is not evident why the pitch contours are implicit, though in these words the vowels are prolonged and the syllables must be necessarily voiced.

5 This complementary explanation of 'otoshi-gami' (toilet paper) can be regarded as the Low Paratone defined in Tench (1996).

6 The cause of this concentration of the low pitches may be that there are only four frequencies indicated in the *praat* software, aside from the exceptional high frequencies over 400 Hz, which are in contradiction with the auditory impression.

CHAPTER 7

Chinese Particles

7.1 Introduction

As a typical tone language, intonation of Chinese does not function in the inter-personal metafunction as in English. In that regard, the Chinese phonological system represented by tone is connected with the levels of lexicon, not that of clause.

Beijing Mandarin[1], referred to as *Putonghua* in Mainland China, distinguishes four tones idiosyncratic to each of *Hanzi* or Chinese character, and the reduced tone *qingsheng* — literally, *light voice*[2]. In one sense, tone languages, represented by Chinese, can not depend on the intonation system to express interpersonal nuances, since the move in pitch is reserved for the lexicon. This should be testified with other tone languages.

Being one of such tone languages, Chinese is similar to Japanese in that both of them depend on sentence-final particles to verbalize interpersonal nuances. But Japanese depends on an intonation system to some extent in distinguishing semantic differences of declarative — interrogative and interrogative — imperative, as reviewed in chapter 5.

There are three subcategories in Chinese particles: structural, manner and SFP[3]. Of the three, only the last one focusing on the mood structure is concerned here. The following description about SFP is from Shang, Hishinuma et al. (1992: 1937, my translation):

> The sentence-final particles directly reflect the speakers' attitude on the occasion of the utterances, undertaking the expression of the emotional and sensitive aspects in addition to the ideational meanings of the sentence.

As far as looking at this definition, Chinese SFPs are similar to the Japanese counterparts with regard to the syntactic and semantic functions. But it is not always the case that the Japanese and Chinese SFPs are completely equivalent to each other from the semantic and syntactic perspectives.

7.2 Chinese Particles

Altogether 12 SFPs are listed in Shang, Hishinuma et al. (1992: 1937)[4]:

(1) ba, a, ya, ne, na, ma, le, la, lei, lie, lou, lo

One of the phonological peculiarities particular to these particles is that they are pronounced in the qingsheng tone, and that they are always in the terminal positions of the clauses, as exemplified below.

These 12 SFPs can be divided into several groups from the derivational viewpoint. The largest is the one derived from *le: le, la, lei, lie, lou, lo*. Most of them are compounds of *le* (phonetically [lə][5]) and monosyllabic interjection-like particles, as follows:

(2) la = le + a, lie = le + ei, lou = le + ou, lo = le + o

So many compounds are formed with *le* might be related to the fact that *le* is rather an aspect marker than a mere SFP, indicating perfective status. In that sense, the compounds in (2) should be regarded as PERFECTIVE + SFP instead of the duplication of SFP + SFP.

Similarly, *na* is a compound of *ne + a*. *A* and *ya* are in complementary distribution (see footnote 20 below), though it may not be always the case.

In the rest of this section, we will look at not all of these 12 particles, due to the restriction of pages, but the typical SFPs as modal embodiment.

Among these 12 SFPs, the interrogative particle *ma* is different from the others in that it is syntactically obligatory whereas the other particles are stylistically optional. In many aspects it is analogous with the Japanese counterpart *ka*, as the following instances illustrate:

(3) ni   qu   ma
     you   go   INTER   'Are you going?'
(4) kimi-wa   iku   ka[6]
     you-TOP   go   INTER   'Are you going?'

The Chinese interrogation (3) can be interchangeable with (5) below without any change in interpersonal nuance, while the Japanese counterpart (6) is syntactically possible, but it is something like an intense questioning:

CHAPTER 7 CHINESE PARTICLES 113

(5) ni qu-bu-qu
        not   'Are you going or not?'
(6) kimi-wa iku ka, ika-nai   ka
                          NEG   'Are you going or not?'

(6) is pragmatically marked, when comparing with the neutral version (4). Japanese can express the interrogative meaning by the rising intonation without *ka*:

(7) kimi-wa iku (with rising intonation)   'Are you going?'

This is in contrast with Chinese which can not have such option since there is no semantic distinction by the sentence intonation.

Ne (phonetically [nə]) is another interrogative particle, but it is used in *wh*-questions, not obligatorily:

(8) zhe   shi   shenme (ne)
     this   COPULA   what   SFP   'What is this?'

By the addition of the SFP *ne*, the intention of quest of information and the nuance of curiosity are more explicit.

Again this is comparable with Japanese *ka*, which is also optional in the *wh*-interrogation:

(9) kore-wa   nan-desu   (ka)
     this-TOP   what-COPULA 'What is this?'

With the existence of the interrogative *nan*[7], the utterance itself is immediately interpreted as a question. In my observation, this expression either with or without *ka* is rather unmarked with a falling intonation; if with a rising, it sounds as if it were purposefully asked. The version without *ka* is stylistically strange to some extent, though it is syntactically adequate.

Though Chinese *ma* and Japanese *ka* have much in common, there is one syntactic disparity; that is, Chinese *ma* is ungrammatical when added to the *wh*-question as in below (my construction)[8], whereas Japanese *ka* is acceptable as shown in (9) above:

(10) *zhe shi shenme ma

The grammatical contrast between (8) and (10) is because of the co-occurrence restriction of *ma* in the *wh*-interrogatives.

As a summary so far in this section, it can be conjectured that Chinese *ma/ne* and Japanese *ka* are parallel in both syntactic and semantic spheres, but it is not the case that both are exactly similar to each other. In Japanese *ka* can terminate an *wh*-interrogation, as instantiated in (9) above.

Besides the above demonstration of the obligatory use of the SFPs *ma* and *ne*, below is the stylistic explanation of the SFPs *a* and *ya*[9] in Shang, Hishinuma et al. (1992: 1937, my translation):

> For example, when replying formally to a senior partner, one should say *shi* 'yes.' When talking in a relaxed mood to each other, however, one can add the SFP *a* or *ya*, and can utter as *shi-a*, *shi-ya*; these styles indicate the direct expression of the open-mindedness as well as frankness between the parties.

It is in one sense strange that the bare form *shi* is politer than the version with *a* or *ya*. Consider the English counterpart 'yes, sir' or 'yes, ma'am' in which the addition of honorifics sound courteous.

Below are further elucidations of the SFP *a* (*op. cit.* p.2):

(11) a. zhe-ci   kaoshi   zhen   nan   a
       this-time   examination   truly   difficult   SFP
       'How difficult is the examination this time!'

    b. wo zhao ta   shi   yinwei youshi   a
       I   visit   him   COPULA   because   be engaged   SFP
       'That I visited him was because I had something to do with him.'

    c. ni   zenme   hai bu qu   a
       you   why   still not go   SPF   'Why haven't you left yet?'

    d. ni a, zhen   you-benshi!
            skillful   'As for you, truly skillful!'

    e. zheli-de shan a,   shui a,   shu a,   cao a,
       here-of   mountain   river   tree   grass
       dou   shi   wo cong-shao   jiu   feichang shuxi-de.
       all   COPULA   since-young   EXPLETIVE[10]   very   familiar
       'The mountains, rivers, trees and grass here, I feel familiar with all of them since I was a child.'

According to the exposition in Shang, Hishinuma *et al.* (1992: 2), (a) is the announcement of exclamation, (b) vindication in the pseudo-cleft form, (c) interrogation suggesting a nuance like 'why on earth,' (d) topicalization or calling attention and (e) listing of things.

In relation to intonation in English, the use of SFP *a* in (11e) above can be compared with what-is-called a listing intonation; that is to say, the SFL *a* is attached to each item listed to indicate that more thing(s) will follow, or some comment is after it. The disaccord is that in English the last entry of the list is realized with the falling tone, whereas *a* is assigned to the last item in Chinese.

Another insightful point with (11e) is that the Japanese counterpart *ya*, though it is a case particle, functions similarly as Chinese *a*:

(12) koko-no   yama-ya,   kawa-ya, ki-ya, kusa-wa, minna tiisai   toki kara
     here-GEN mountain river   tree   grass   all   young time since
     nare-sitasin-de iru
     familiar with   STATE

As well as Chinese *a* in the use (11e) above, Japanese *ya* is not in the sentence-final position. In all of the instances (11a) through (11e), the particle *a* is optional; it can be omitted in all of the above utterances.

Another crucial SFP in Chinese is *ba*, one of the most frequently used particles. We will look at the four major denotations of this particle.

The first uses are for indicating consultation, suggestion, demand, and command.

(13) a. Women kuai   zou ba.
        we   soon   go SFP   'Let's go now.'(suggestion)
     b. Gei   women chang   yi-zhi   ger   ba.
        give   us   sing   one-MEASURE   song   SFP
        'Please sing a song for us.'   (demand)
     c. Bang-bang   ta   ba.
        help   him SFP   'Help him.'   (command)

This first group of usages are the most fundamental significance of *ba*. The versions without it — (a) *women kuai zou*, (b) *gei women chang yi-zhi ger* — they are syntactically correct and will be felt weaker in addressing suggestion or demand to the hearer, though the intentions will be communicated. The reduplication of the verb *bang* in (c) is almost obligatory with the one-syllable verbs.

The second usage is the expression of agreement or approval:

(14) Hao   ba,   wo daying   ni   le.
     OK   SFP   I   undertake you   PERF
     'OK, I will comply with you.'   (agreement)

In (14), *ba* is attached to the monosyllabic adjective *hao* (good), which is in contrast with the three examples in (13) in which it is in the clause-final positions. It will need more consideration whether the sentence-final versions as in (14)′ are possible or not:

(14)′ a. Hao,   wo daying ni le ba
       b. Hao ba, wo daying ni le ba.

In the Japanese counterpart, all of (14) and (14)′ will be translated as follows:

(14)″ Ii-yo,   hikiuketa (yo).
       OK-SFP   undertake   'OK, I will comply with you.'

Whereas the first *yo* is obligatory, the second one is not. This is because the sharing of the information is stronger with the first one than in the second one. In other words, the action of undertaking something belongs to the doer, and in that sense it is a personal matter rather than interpersonal.

The next implication is interrogative and guessing:

(15) Zhe-ban   huoche   bu   hui   wan-dian   ba.
     this-MEASURE   train   not   may   be late   SFP
     'This train should not be late, should it?'

This utterance is to intend to ascertain that the train would not be late. The addition of the SFP *ba* strongly presupposes the existence of the hearer, since it should be unnatural without *ba*, even though it is uttered to the speaker himself/herself.

As well as *a* and *ya*, *ba* is sometimes in the midst of clauses. In such cases, the label *sentence-final* is slightly unsuitable. The resolution in Shang, Hishinuma et al. (1992: 26) for (16) is intricate; the whole clause consists of antithesis, and each of them is with *ba*:

(16) Zou ba, bu   hao,   bu zou ba, ye bu hao.
     go   SFP not good   also
     'If I should go, it is not good; if I should not, it is not good, either.'[11]

In the first half of (16), the verb is positive and in the second half negative; the

CHAPTER 7 CHINESE PARTICLES

polarity of the adjective *hao* is reversed — negative in the former and positive in the latter, thus making an antithesis. In this contrast of polarity, SFP *ba* is predominant in the rhetoric effect in this particular case.

As a problem to be solved in the next occasions, I would point out that Chinese particles listed so far in this section correspond to the Japanese SFPs and case particles. This would be due to a syntactic variable that there is no equivalent in Chinese to Japanese case particles, hence its use is undertaken by *a*, as exhibited in the example (11e).

Notes

1 Mandarin is currently the most prestigious dialect in not only Mainland China but also in Taiwan, and Hong Kong after its return from Britain.

2 For the introductory description of the four tones and *qingsheng*, see Kadooka (1998b: 233).

3 Chinese traditional term for this third category is *yuqi-zhuzi*: mood particle. As will be elaborated in the main text, it has much in common with the Japanese SFPs. Mainly for the purpose of the unification with the Japanese grammar, it will be referred to as *SFP* throughout the discussion in this paper.

4 The Chinese examples in this section are from this dictionary unless otherwise mentioned. Romanization is based on the Pin'yin system, though tone critics above the vowel symbols will be omitted.

5 This use as a particle *le* is a reduced form of a full verb *liao* (to finish), with the lenition of the vowel and the tone; as a verb it has the third tone.

6 It is unmarked for this utterance with rising intonation. If it is said with a falling intonation, it is felt like the self consent, not addressing the partner in the conversation.

7 Etymologically this form *nan* derives from more formal *nani*. In this particular case, *nani* is not interchangeable with *nan*: " *kore-wa nani desu-ka*. It will be another topic why *nani* is not appropriate here.

8 Some exceptions to the co-occurrence restriction are instanced in Shang, Hishinuma *et al.* (1992: 1002), in which *shei* and *shenme* designate some particular person or thing, respectively:

a. shei   dou   zhidao ma   b. ni   xiang mai xie   shenme ma
   who   all   know   you think buy some   what
   'Does anyone know (it)?'   'Do you want to buy something?'

9 Shang, Hishinuma et al. (1992: 1669) mention that *ya* is in complementary distribution with *a* in that the former appears following the vowel sounds.

10 *Jiu* is originally an adverb with the meaning 'immediately; at once,' and the use as an expletive derives from this.

11 Just as in a Japanese subjectless case (14a), the subject of this can be interpreted as 'you.'

CHAPTER 8

CV Variations and Relative Productivity

8.1 Introduction

It was suggested in Kadooka (1996a, 1996b) that the number of the syllable variations in a given language is related to the combinations and the order of the consonants and vowels as syllable structure, as well as the inventories of the phonemes of vowels and consonants. Here the notion *syllable structure* designates the phonotactic combinations and arrangement of vowels (V) and consonants (C), such as V, CV, CVC, and will be referred to as the CV *variations* hereafter. In this chapter, the relation between syllable structure and CV variations will be disputed from typological viewpoints, citing the data from various languages.

Kadooka (1996a, 1996b) also suggest that it would be appropriate to classify the languages of the world into three groups with regard to the number of syllable inventories: the first group are consisted of the languages with less than 100 syllables; the second group 101 to 1000; and the third one more than 1000. This tripartite will reveal various phonological features within and across each of the groups. The first group contains languages such as Hawaiian, whose phoneme inventory is extremely small. The second group consists of more various languages than in the first one: Japanese, Chinese and so on. The languages belonging to the third group, probably the distribution will be restricted than the second group, present the most complicated phonological structures.

One of the phonological difference related with this tripartite is the distribution of consonant clusters (henceforth abbreviated as C *clusters*). There is no C clusters found in the languages of the first group. In the languages with a few hundred to one thousand syllables, on the other hand, limited combinations of C clusters are possible in certain position, mostly syllable-terminal. The languages with more than one thousand syllables permit fairly free types of C clusters both in syllable-initial and-terminal positions. This issue will be sketched in Section 2.

Glides (G) can be dichotomized into onglides and offglides. Definitionally, those syllables only with onglide are treated as /CV/, while those only with off-glide are /V/. In other words, the sequence /VG/ is a diphthong and considered as a kind of 'vowel cluster.' The more detailed investigation can be done by distinguishing glides in classifying CV variations.

The onglides such as /y, w/ will not be regarded as part of the phoneme inventory of the onset consonant /#C-/. Instead they will be considered to be part of the quality of the nuclear vowels; /y/ is a glide featuring palatality, while /w/ a fearture of labiality. French glide /ɥ/ as in *huit* /ɥit/ (eight) contains both palatality and labiality at the same time.

Relative productivity, first suggested in Trnka (1968:112ff), is the second phonological feature related with the syllable inventory. On the one hand, complicated patterns of C clusters multiply the number of the types of possible syllables in a given language. On the other hand, however, the actual syllables found among the languages, typically those of the third group above, present only a part of such possible phoneme combinations. As a consequence, therefore, the relative productivity of the syllables, especially those with complicated C cluster patterns, is low. This topic of RP will be focused during the discussion in Section 3.

The most important purpose of this chapter is to exemplify that the size of syllable inventory and the relative productivity is interrelated: the greater the syllable inventory in a given language, is the lower the relative productivity is, as is the typical case with English; if the language has the small syllable inventory, to the contrary, its relative productivity should be greater in order to make the most use of the fewer syllable variations, as in Hawaiian. The intermediate cases are again Japanese and Chinese.

8.2 CV Variations

In this section, it will be considered crosslinguistically which of the phonological variables such as numbers of phonemes, phonotactics or other factors are related to the size of syllable inventories.

To put in an extremely simple way, the more phonemes a given language contains, the more syllable variations. In one way of the merest calculation, the number of the syllable types is the result of the multiplication of the numbers of vowels and consonants, with the manner of phonotactic arrangements of CV variations considered.

Actually, there are some *phonological gaps* in the lexicon in any language. It should be necessary to distinguish two types of phonological gaps: structural gaps and accidental gaps. *Structural gaps* are those in which certain sequences of phonemes are systematically prohibited in a given language. In accidental gaps, as the term indicates, a given arrangement of the phonemes are phonotactically permitted but lacks its realization in the existing lexicon. A well known example of English accidental gap is /blik/ *vis-à-vis* a structural gap /bnik/: the onset C cluster of a plosive followed by a nasal is phonologically entirely impossible, as in the latter. The accidental gap /blik/, on the other hand, is phonotactically permissible in English phonology, but it lacks a lexical realization[1]. Both of these types of gaps should be subtracted from the mere multiplication of vowel and consonant phonemes for the syllable inventory to be consistent with the lexicon.

However, the matter is not so simple when contrasting the syllable inventories across languages of the different families. As shown in Kadooka (1996a, 1996b), the ratio of the number of syllables of Hawaiian to that of English is much greater than that of the phonemes in these two languages. The difference is twice with vowels (10:20) and nearly three times with the consonants (8:22), and the mere combinations of the vowel and consonant phonemes, therefore, render the difference of only six times as the simple multiplication of the both. The actual difference of syllable inventories, about 40 times between the two languages, should be ascribed to the number of the CV variations in each language. In Kadooka (1996a:43) it has been testified that there are only two variations in Hawaiian while 14 for English, the difference amounting to as many as seven times, which may be the greatest possiblity to answer the question above.

Therefore arises the need to take the CV variations into account in order to explicate the gap between the syllable inventories and the number of the phonemes cross-linguistically. Below are the chart to contrast the CV variations of the seven languages of different origin; Hawaiian is one of the Polynesian languages of the Central Pacific; Chinese, in this case Beijing Mandarin, a representative of SinoTibetan; Korean and Japanese, both would be interrelated, though the origin of neither has been testified yet; Mundari is one of 'Austroasiatic' languages (see below); Sandawe is spoken in South Africa, belonging to the Bantu language family; and English being one of the Germanic languages:

(1)

Hawaiian	Chinese	Korean	Japanese	Mundari	Sandawe	English
V	V	V	V	V	V	
CV	CV	CV	CV	CV	CV	CV
	VC	VC	VC	VC	VC	VC
	CVC	CVC	CVC	CVC	CVC	CVC
						VCC
					CCV	CCV
			(CVCC)			CVCC

```
                    CCVC
                    CCCV
                        CVCCC
                    CCVCC
                    CCCVC
                        CCVCCC
                    CCCVCC
```

The indication /V/ can represent the only one type of vowel, but ideally long vowels and diphthongs should be distinguished typographically so that more minute comparison be possible.

First, before the discussion of the contrast among these languages, some notice will be necessary for the explanation of each of the individual languages.

'Chinese' designates Beijing Mandarin among many dialects within and outside Mainland China. Data is mainly from Kadooka (1990).

The parenthized syllable type (CVCC) in Japanese denotes superheavy syllables of three morae with geminate consonants. Such extralong syllables are indicated by bold types in the data below, adding the examples of long vowels followed by the third mora /Q/ or /N/:

(2) a. [**toot**.ta][2] b. [aan]   c. [ron.**donk**.ko]
     /**tooQ**.ta/   /aRN/   /roN.**doNQ**.ko/
     pass PAST   (the manner of opening   London child (lit.)
     'passed'   one's mouth wide)   'Londoner'

The first syllable of (2a) /tooQ/ contains a long vowel followed by a moraic consonant /Q/; in (b) /aRN/ is one syllable, with the long vowel /aR/ preceding a moraic nasal /N/; the second syllable of (2c) is two-mora /doN/ also followed by /Q/. These three-mora superheavy syllables can be indicated uniformly as /CVXC/ where /X/ signifies both /C/ and /R/. As is clear from the above examples in (2), Japanese three-mora superheavy syllables are found among the conjugated verb form (a) or suffixed foreign loan words (c). The phonetic entity of the 'long vowel' in the conjugated predicate in (a) needs cautious examination since it may be two syllables, whereas the derived noun from place names as in (c) is limited to foreign loan words ending with /N/, since there is only a few place names terminated with the nasal consonant (e. g. Muroran). Considering the principle in Trnka (1968) that the derivations be excluded from the 'authentic' CV variaiton (see below), the status of these three-mora syllables is dubious. Whether this syllable type /CVXC/ should be included in the inveontory is suspended at the moment, though the conclusion would be likely to deny it.

In Mundari, one of the 'Austroasiatic' languages (see Osada (1992:1516) for the detail of this classification of the language), /V/ never appears in monosyllabic lexion; in the disyllabic words, there are vowel sequences consisted of two independent sinlge vowels /V.V/ such as /a.u/ (to bring).

Some regularity and differences across languages are immediately known from the table above. The syllable type /CV/ is common among the listed languages, and probably all the languages of the world. On the other hand, the simplest form of /V/ is not found in Sandawe, one of the Bantu languages. In Sandawe, the vowels in monosyllables should be preceded by a glottal stop, therefore the type /V/ does not exist.

The type /CVC/ can be found among the languages in (1) above except in Hawaiian, so it would be possible to regard it fairly universal crosslinguistically. Common though it is, the coda consonant /C/ of this variation presents somewhat different distribution from one language to another. In Chinese, this /C/ is limited to nasal /n, ŋ/; in Japanese it is realized either as moraic nasal /N/ or as moraic consonant /Q/, and so on. In English, contrastively, the member of the coda consonants are almost identical with those of the onset consonants. The only exception is /ŋ/ which cannot begin a syllable.

It is evident as well that English contains the most complicated CV variation system among (1) above: altogether 14 of them, which is overwhelmingly more numerous than the other languages considered. In the list (1), English was chosen as the representative of the Indo-European language family, and it may be surmised that Indo-European languages on the whole present a similar tendency as English with regard to CV variations. Now, then, let us try the same kind of contrast as (1) above within the Indo-European languages:

(3)

English	Dutch	French	Spanish	Welsh	Modern Greek
V	V	V	V	V	V
CV	CV	CV	CV	CV	CV
VC	VC	VC	VC	VC	VC
CVC	CVC	CVC	CVC	CVC	CVC
VCC	VCC	VCC	VCC		
CCV	CCV	CCV	CCV	CCV	CCV
	VCCC				
CVCC	CVCC	CVCC		CVCC	
CCVC	CCVC	CCVC	CCVC	CCVC	
CCCV	CCCV	CCCV		CCCV	
	VCCCC				
CVCCC	CVCCC			CVCCC	
CCVCC	CCVCC	CCVCC		CCVCC	
CCCVC	CCCVC	CCCVC		CCCVC	
	CVCCCC				
CCVCCC	CCVCCC	CCVCCC			

CCCVCC   CCCVCC   CCCVCC   CCCVCC

In general, contrary to the expectation, the languages of different branches within the Indo-European family present two-polar tendency represented by Dutch and Modern Greek. The one polar is the one like Dutch, in which varieties of CV patterns are exemplified, and the other is like Modern Greek which rather looks like Japanese or Chinese.

The four-consonant clusters in Dutch are attested with the words such as *ernst* /ɛrnst/ (English *earnest*) and *herfst* /hɛrfst/ (*autumn*, related to English *harvest* and German *Herbst* /hɛrpst/). In the English counterparts /ɔː.nist/ and /hɑː.vist/, epenthetic vowel /i/ renders another syllable avoiding the four-consonant cluster. Notice although that in English the similar four-consonant cluster is exemplified with the suffixed forms such as 'sixths' /siksθs/, which is not recognized as 'authentic' in Trnka (1968). Following such line, the status of the variation with the consonant geminate as of /CVCC/ in Japanese is highly dubious.

Further, it can be pointed out that Dutch patterns such as /VCCC/, /VC-CCC/, /CVCCCC/ are unique which are not observed in English.

Both in French and Welsh, syllable-terminal three C cluster /-CCC#/ is testified but rare, while the similar cluster appear quite commonly in syllable-initial positions /#CCC-/. French *spectre* /spɛktr/ (specter) and Welsh *priddlestr* /prid.lestr/ (earthenware vessel), *bustl* /bustl/ (gall, bile), *callestr* /ka.lestr/ (flint), are found but exceptional.

Greek /#V#/ type syalble is exemplified but exceptional in that /V/ does not constitute monosyllabic lexicon.

In conclusion, the Germanic langauges offer more various CV types among Indo-European family. This is attested by the syllable-terminal three C cluster /-CCC#/. Other languages of non-Germanic origin basically do not permit such complicated C cluster in the coda position.

8.3 Relative Productivity

Under the tradition of the Structuralism through the twentieth century, phonology of the various languages had been cast significant light by the scholars of Bloomfieldian and Prague school linguists. Trnka (1968) is one of the representative works of the Structuralism analysis of modern English from the perspective of syllable structures.

Trnka (1968:112) presents the figure of *relative productivity* (henceforth RP) for all of the 14 CV variations of English. The figures designate the actual occurrences of syllable within the greatest possible number of the combinations of the phonemes. The type with the largest productivity is /V/: 11 syllables testified among 14 vowel phonemes[3], the RP being 78.57%. The smallest occurrence is those with the structure of /CCVCCC/, 3 out of 6080 possibilities or 0.05%. The total possibility is 89,165 while the actual occurrence is 3203, hence the productivity is only 3.50%. Such a low rate of productivity of English is partly due to various phonotactic constraints, for instance the first consonant of the syllable-initial three C cluster is /s/. In addition, we can observe a tendency that the more phonemes a given CV variation contains, the lower RP.

Young (1992:46), on the other hand, presents another interesting calculation for the English syllable inventory: the mere multiplications of 22 onset consonants, 19 nucleus vowels, and 18 terminal consonants amount to 7,524. This is the surmise of the syllable type CVC. As for this type, there are 1346 syllables of that structure, which is the most prevalent of all the CV types (Trnka (1968:111)); but the RP is 17.88%. That is to say, more than four fifths of the combinations of /CVC/ phonemes are inappropriate and excluded in the English lexicon.

It can be concluded that the RP of English syllable inventory is low, which may reflect the abundance of CV variations and C clusters. In the syllable-initial C clusters, for instance, the more the numbers of phonemes, the more restricted is the order and arrangement of them. The greatest possible initial cluster is /#CCC-/ and the first consonant should be /s/, as is well known. Similar kind of restrictions are true with regard to the syllable terminal C clusters such as in /CVCCC/.

Contrary to that the languages with greater syllable inventories present low RP, the languages with smaller inventories will offer high RP. Take Hawaiian for example. Hawaiian is known to be a language with quite a small set of phonemes. It is especially evident with the consonants of only eight phonemes. Five vowels are distinguished by the length, rendering altogether 10 phonemes. The total number of syllables in Hawaiian is 90 including the syllables with zero-initials, as shown in Kadooka (1996a:36, 44). Therefore, the Hawaiian language must make the most use of the small syllable inventory, otherwise too many words would be realized with the same phonetic representations.

In the rest of this section, the phoneme inventories, CV variations and RP in Korean, Japanese and Chinese will be reviewed on the basis of the discussion up to now.

8.3.1 Korean

There are 22 consonants which can occupy syllable-initial position, 21 vocoids and seven consonants that can close the syllables. The calculation is to multiply

126

23 onsets including the zero consonant, 21 nuclei and 8 codas including zero consonant in which case the syllable is open: the result is 3,864. Needless to say, these 21 nuclei do not happen equally; those with onglides would be less frequent than those without.

There are 22 consonant phonemes in Korean distinguished in the syllable-initial position; among them, nine archiphonemes /k, n, t, r, m, p, s, tʃ, h/ are discerned. The three plosives /k, t, p/ and an affricate /tʃ/ have geminated and aspirated allophones respectively, while /s/ has only the geminated allophone /ʔs/:

(4)   k   t   p   tʃ   s   r   m   n   h
     ʔk   ʔt   ʔp   ʔtʃ   ʔs
     kʰ   tʰ   pʰ   tʃʰ

The phonetic descriptions of these phonemes are as follows: /k, n, t, s, tʃ/ are weak voiceless aspirated in the morpheme-initial positions, and voiced between the voiced sounds; /ʔk, ʔt, ʔp, ʔtʃ, ʔs/ are voiceless unaspirated anywhere; /kʰ, tʰ, pʰ, tʃʰ/ are strong voiceless aspirated (Umeda (1989:951), though the phonetic symbols are otherwise indicated).

These allophones render phonological minimal pairs, and orthographically they are added special symbols to the archiphonemes. Voiceless aspirated sounds are added one stroke to the consonant alphabets of archiphonemes, whereas they are reduplicated with unaspirated counterpart.

/ŋ/ occurs only in syllable-terminal positions and is assigned the same symbol as that of syllable-initial consonant /h/, which shows that the Hangul, the Korean orthography invented in the fifteeenth century, utilizes the concept of the complementary distribution of the phonemes /h/ and /ŋ/. In that sense as well, Korean orthography is highly phonology-conscious.

On the other hand, contrary to the onset position, only seven consonants can occupy the syllableterminal position: /p, t, k, m, n, ŋ, l/.

Arranged in the manner of the traditional vowel chart, the basic vowel system of Korean is presented as follows (Umeda (1989:952)):

(5)   i   ɯ   u
     e   ə   o
     ɛ   a   ɔ

This chart indicates that nine vowel phonemes should be distinguished as basic vowels, which is inconsistent with the otrthography.

In the Hangul orthography, six vowels are regarded as basic one: /a, ɔ, o, u, ɯ, i/. When the onglide /j/ are added to the four of them, one stroke is added to the original fonts respectively: /ja, jɔ, jo, ju/. The rest of the vocoid sounds are the combinations of these ten symbols:

(6) /ɛ/ : /a/ + /i/   /jɛ/ : /ja/ + /i/   /wa/ : /o/ + /a/
    /wɛ/ : /o/ + /a/ + /i/   /we/ : /o/ + /i/   /wi/ : /u/ + /i/
    /e/ : /ɔ/ + /i/   /je/ : /jɔ/ + /i/   /wɔ/ : /u/ + /ɔ/
    /we/ : /u/ + /ɔ/ + /i/   /ɯi/ : /ɯ/ + /i/

It will be immediately clear from this table that the simplex vowel /e/ and /ɛ/ are indicated as the intermediate with regard to the tongue height of /ɔ/ and /i/, and /a/ and /i/, respectively. In other words, /e/ and /ɛ/ are orthographically regarded as compound. Those with onglides are the orthographical and phonological combinations of more than two sounds/symbols. Though it seems complicated and cumbersome at first, the Hangul vowel transcriptions are extremely systematic.

Up to this stage, the material is not available as for the syllable inventory of Korean, so the discussion must be postponed until the next occasion when it is ready.

8.3.2 Japanese

The CV variations of Japanese are characteristic in that the syllables of two morae are formulated by adding either moraic nasal /N/, moraic consonant /Q/ or the prolongation of the vowel /R/, and three-mora syllables by /R/ and either /Q/ or /N/ (Kadooka (1996b:45)). In that sense, two-and three-mora syllables form-other layers on that of one-mora basic syllables. In other words, two-or three-mora syllables should have their one-mora sylalble counterparts.

The three-mora pattern /CVRQ/ is confined to those lexicon of onomatopoeia, as in the following examples:

(7) a. kaRQ   to   naru
       the manner of anger CITATION   become   'to get angry'
    b. kura-kuraRQ to kuru
       dizzy   come   'be dizzy'

These forms, however, should be necessarily followed by the citation particle *to*. In that sense they are not productive.

In (7a) above, the manner adverbial 'kaRQ' can be contrasted with the short-vowel counterpart 'kaQ'; the short-vowel version suggests the momentarity of the feeling of anger, whereas in 'kaRQ' it is more continuous. Such semantic differentiation can not be distinguished between (7b) 'kura-kuraRQ' and its short-vowel version 'kura-kuraQ' where it can be maintained that the former is an emphatic form of the latter.

There are 12 consonant phonemes in Japanese: /p, b, t, d, k, g, s, z, r-m, n, h/. Together with five vowel phonemes /i, e, a, o, u/, the inventory of one-mora syllables amounts to 65, including zero initials. Of the five vowels above, three back ones /a, o, u/ are palatalized, forming other 39 syllables (13 x 3). Among these 104 syllables, four pairs are orthographically distinguished but homophonous[4]:

(8) /zi//di/ [dʒi]   /zu//du/ [dzu]   /zya//dya/ [dʒa]   /zyo//dyo/ [dʒo]

Subtracting these homophones and adding /wa/ render 101 basic syllables.

These 101 basic syllables are for the native lexicon. As Shirota (1993) argues in detail, however, loan phonology has been introduced realizing such phonetic forms as [tiː] ('tea') and the first syllable of [ʃeːkaː] ('shaker'). It can be concluded that this kind of phonological innovation is quite ordinary among younger generation.

Following are such innovatory syllables mainly found among foreign loanwords:

(9) /she tye tsa tse tso ti   tu dye dyu   di   du/
     [ʃe tʃe tsa tse tso ti   tu dʒe dʒu   di   du]

These 11 syllables are permissible in the Japanese phonotactics as compared with those in (10) below in that the former are of the format of one mora basic syllable while those of the latter are not. Adding to the 101 syllable variations considered above, there are 112 syllable variations in Japanese.

Notice that 'orthographical diphthongs' /ou/ and /ei/ are phonetically monophthongized as [oː] and [eː] respectively in the Sino-Japanese and native lexicon. Among the loan words of Western languages written with *Katakana*, these sounds are transcribed with the prolongation symbol '—,' thus nearer to the phonetic entities of these sounds.

In syllable-terminal consonants of the constituent of the geminate, the feature [+voiced] is marked from the articulatory viewpoint in Japanese. The moraic consonant /Q/ as in a phonological transcription, represents the glottis constriction in the phonetic realization with any obstruent. Therefore it induces some difficulty of voicing compared with voiceless consonant. These configurations are, therefore, exclusively limited to the loanwords from Western langauges, such as follows:

CHAPTER 8 CV VARIATIONS AND RELATIVE PRODUCTIVITY 129

(10) /sutaQbu   beQdo   baQgu   suraQgaR   biQgu/
    [su.tab.bu   bed.do   bag.gu   su.rag.gaa   big.gu]
    stab   bed   bag   slagger   big

As for English *bag*, there is one lexical entry whose CV pattern is the same as this but different in Japanese: *bug*. It is only pronounced as [ba.gu] without /Q/, so it seemingly makes minimal pair with [bag.gu].

There found some lexical items unstable as for the insertion of /Q/ as follows:

(11) /no(Q)bu   ue(Q)bu   ki(Q)su/
    [no(b).bu   u.e(b).bu   ki(s).su]
    knob   web   kiss

This state of affairs tells that the value [+voiced] for /Q/ is unnatural in Japanese phonology in general.

This is testified by the fact that the following words are pronounced and/or transcribed by the native speakers of Japanese as the following:

(12) /baQku/ for *bag*   /biQku/ for *big*   /beQto/ for *bed*
    バック   ビック   ベット

Considering that this pattern of /Q/:[+voiced] is phonologically irregular and lacks productivity except in the syllable forms /(C)VQC/, and that native lexicon never permit this pattern because of this phonotactic restriction, this configuration should be excluded from the syllable inventory of Japanese.

Now, at last, let us look at the RP of Japanese in each of the CV variations. RP is deduced from the existential syllables among 112 basic ones. Below is the table showing the figure with my own intuition:

(13)

type	subtype	occurrences	RP (%)
CV		110	98.2
	CVV	109	97.3
CVC	CVN	97	86.6
	CVp	73	65.2
	CVt	88	78.6
	CVk	85	75.9
	CVs	66	58.9
	CVh	23	20.5
CVRN		75	67.0
CVRQ		43	38.4
total		769	68.7

This is the result of the scrutiny of each syllable in Japanese. Here there being no space to list all of the result of the investigation, it should be noticed that it may need refinement. The total combination patterns of Japanese syllables amount to 1120, the basis of the calculation of the RP.

8.3.3 Chinese

When looking at the syllable chart of Mandarin Chinese as in Kadooka (1990: 63, 64), the Relative Productivity is visibly recognized at a glance.

The consonant and vowel phonemes of Beijing Mandarin is as follows (the Pin'yin phonemic representations are adopted):

(14) p t k s sh   c ch   q x f l r h m n   i ü u
     b d g z zh   j   e o
                                                a

Notice that the consonants /g, k, h/ and /j, q, x/ are in complementary distribution in the table above: /g, k, h/ are followed by back vowels /u, e, a/[5] while the latter pairs /j, q, x/ by front vowels /i, ü/. Vowels are phonologically classified into six phonemes: /i, ü, u, ə, o, a/. These basic vowels are optionally combined with onglides /i, ü, u/, offglides /i, o, u/ and consonantal endings /n, ŋ/ (see Kadooka (1990:35) for the detail of the phonetic representations of these Mandarin sounds), thus forming 34 variations of the rhyme. Following are the patterns of the rhyme of Mandarin Chinese (from Kadooka (1990:51)[6]:

(15) V   offG   onG   on & offG   N   onG & N
     /a/   a ai ao   ia ua   iao uai   an aŋ   ian iaŋ   uan uaŋ   üan
     /e/   e   ie ui ue   en eŋ
     /o/   ou   uo   oŋ   ioŋ
     /i/   yi   in iŋ
     /u/   wu   iu   un
     /ü/   yu   ün

As Pin'yin transcription, /#i-, #u-, #ü-, -ŋ#/ are indicated as /yi, wu, yu, ng/ respectively. The examples of the first three morphemes are: /yi/ (one), /wu/ (five), /yu/ (rain).

Schematically, the rhyme types in (15) are: /V, VG, GV, GVG, VN, GVN/, in which nasals /n, ŋ/ indicated as /N/. Those vowels with the offglide are diphthongs, i.e. /-VG, -GVG/, and the syllables with these diphthongs belong to the variation /(C)V/. Those syllables with nasals (N), on the other hand, are the type /(C)VC/. In Beijing Mandarin there is a cooccurrence restriction of offglide followed by a nasal, i.e. */(C)VGN/.

There can be distinguished 15 rhyme patterns in the above table including the type /V/. With each vowel these 15 patterns can be formulated, therefore the number of the total possible occurrences is 90. The actual combinations are 32, however. The RP concluded from these figures is 35.56%. This is the first step to calculate the RP in Chinese.

Instead of counting syllable variations in the manner for English as in Trnka (1968), the number of the possible syllables is known immediately and so is the combinations of onset and rhyme in the case of Mandarin. The multiplication of 19 onset consonants including zero and 34 rhyme variations results 646 variations. The actual syllable occurrings are 409, the RP of Mandarin Chinese being 63.31% as a whole.

This figure is relatively high, partly because the possible types of rhyme are predetermined in (15). The syllable table as in Kadooka (1990:63,64) is based on such rhyme patterns.

Compared with Japanese, it would be possible to conclude that Chinese phonotactics is not flexible in the sense that nonse syllables like /myo/ or /pyaan/ cannot be transcribed because there is no corresponding character to represent the sound.

8.4 Conclusion

In this chapter, it has been tried to exemplify crosslinguistically that the size of the syllable inventory and the RP is interrelated. Though the discussion was a sketchy one, some tendency was suggested that the greater the syllable inventory, the smaller the RP in a given language. Because the detailed investigation of the syllable inventory in any language needs more pages, enlarged study will be necessary.

Below is the table contrasting the three languages of English, Chinese, and Japanese as for the syllable inventory and RP:

(16)	language	number of syllables	RP (%)
	English	3203	3.50
	Japanese	769	68.7
	Chinese	409	63.31

The RP of Japanese and Chinese are almost similar, both much greater than that of English, approximately 20 times. The difference between the two groups is as predicted with the introduction of the concept of RP.

132

Further, it is probable that Dutch, with more CV variations than English, contains greater syllable inventory and the RP is lower than any other languages in (16), and that Hawaiian, whose syllable inventory includes 90 of all, is the opposite case.

This polarization tendency will be fortified with the data from more languages of diverse origin.

Notes

1 In the same language family of the Germanic as English, a Dutch word /blik/ (tin) is an existential phonological combination.

2 A full stop indicates the syllable boundary in the phonetic transcriptions.

3 These 14 vowel phonemes are: nine diphthongs /iə, uə, ɛə, ɔə, ei, ai, oi, ou, au/ and five long vowels /iː, uː, əː, ɑː, ɔː/. As for the six basic vowels /i, ɛ, a, ɑ, ɔ, u/, they are not taken into consideration because they can not constitute syllables without onset and coda consonant in monosyllabic lexicon.

4 The phonetic symbols here, those of the consonants in particular, tentatively follows those of IPA, mainly from the typographical reasons.

5 The phonetic entity of Mandarin /e/ is near to [ə], therefore its distinctive feature being [front] rather than [+front].

6 There are some transcription differences in the Pin'yin system between the syllables with and without onset consonant: /ui/ /#wei/, /oŋ/ /#weng/, /iu/ /#you/, /un/ /#wen/. See Kadooka (1990:64) for the detail of these sounds.

CHAPTER 9

Conclusion

Here is the table summarizing the analyses of the languages shown in Chapter 2:

(1)

language	lexicon	clause intonation
American English	stress accent	larger
British English	stress accent	larger
German	stress accent	larger
Dutch	stress accent	larger
Swedish	stress+pitch accent	larger
Danish	stress accent	larger
Spanish	stress accent	larger
European Portuguese	stress accent	larger
Brazil Potuguese	stress accent	larger
French	stress accent	larger
Italian	stress accent	larger
Romanian	stress accent	larger
Russian	stresss accent	larger
Bulgarian	stress accent	larger
Greek	stress accent	larger
Finnish	stress accent	limited
Hungarian	stress accent	limited
Western Arabic	stress accent	unknown
Japanese	pitch accent	limited
Thai	tone language	more limited

Vietnamese	tone language	more limited
Beijing Mandarin	tone language	more limited

The most conspicuous finding in terms of the tripartite tone language/stress accent/pitch accent is the scarceness of the pitch accent system languages; there are only two languages of Japanese and Swedish. Though it is a major system in Japanese, it is subsidiary in Swedish. In summary, the stress accent system is definitely predominant vis-à-vis pitch accent system. It seems necessary from a typological viewpoint to find other example of pitch accent system other than Japanese.

The next point is the distinction of the function of clause intonation: larger and limited. As shown with the examples in chapter 2, the function of clause intonation is literally limited in tone languages. That of the pitch accent system languages, however, is relatively limited compared to those of the stress accent system languages. It is relative in the sense that the pragmatic nuances lack in the former. In order to deal with this difference, the function of clause intonation is labelled as *more limited*.

Summarizing the contrast among the three languages attested so far is the table below, adding the syntactic categories which have not been subject here, such as the classical tripartite inflectional/agglutinative/isolating and the word order of subject, verb and object. The shadowed items are the principal means for communicating interpersonal nuances:

Table 9.1: Typology of syntax and pragmatics

	English	Japanese	Chinese
typological class	inflectional	agglutinative	isolating
word order	SVO	SOV	SVO
wh-interrogatives	initial	free	free
modal auxiliaries	+	+	+
accent pattern	stress	pitch	tone
intonation	++	+	–
SFP	±[1]	+	+
tag question	+	–	–
exclamation	+	–	–

Though modal auxiliaries are indicated as common to three languages, the other categories vary from one language to another. Other than modal auxiliaries, intonation, tag question, and exclamation are highlighted in English, whereas it is SFPs in Japanese and Chinese. It is insightful that SFPs play a crucial role as pragmatic nuance carrier in Japanese and Chinse, though these languages are different typologically.

If we look at this table without scrutinizing the data in each language, the conclusion may be that 'Japanese and Chinese SFPs assume interpersonal nuances instead of English intonation,' which is not always the case. This is true to some extent, but the correspondences among the three languages are not straightforward, as shown in a figure 4.1 below.

The tripartite stress/pitch/tone for the rubric *accent pattern* may be controversial. On the one hand, English and Japanese are in contrast with the accent patterns of stress and pitch, respectively; these are relative criteria in stressed—unstressed, high—low, respectively. On the other hand, Chinese is a tone language whereas neither English nor Japanese is; a tone language is an absolute concept that some particular contour is attached to each lexical item. This is another theme for the future development.

Tench (1996: 21–23) exemplifies the minimal pairs of the tonality, under the rubric of 'syntactic structure':

(2) a. He *asked* himself
    b. He asked him*self* [2]

In (2a), the verb *asked* is transitive while its counterpart in (2b) is intransitive; in (2a) the action was self-questioning, and (2b) implies that 'he himself asked (to someone), no one else did the asking.'

Let us look at another amusing pair of the tonality in Tench (1996: 22):

(3) a. *Cut* yourself.
    b. Cut your*self*.

(3a) is syntactically unmarked but semantically marked, and in (3b) vice versa. (3a) is telling that the addresser commands the addressee to wound himself/herself; (3b) is to intend to ask the hearer to cut the cake himself/herself.

Below is a diagram depicting the interrelations of the functional categories of the three languages; but the relation between English and Chinese is not attested, hence not indicated. The arrow denotes the dependent direction — e.g. English intonation and Japanese SFPs are interdependent or bilateral, whereas Japanese SFPs depends on English prominence unidirectionally:

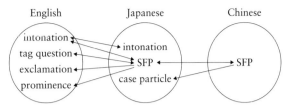

Figure 9.1: Correspondence between languages

Notice again that these listed categories are not thoroughgoing; this is only a hinting illustration, needing more pursuit.

It would be more intriguing if we distinguished the degree of correspondence with, for instance, the width of the lines between the categories. Then it would be apparent which relation is predominant and which is subsidiary. The most conspicuous is that the two categories of SFPs in Japanese and Chinese would be related to each other noticeably.

There seem to be two ways of the future direction. On the one hand, each system — English intonation, Japanese and Chinese SFPs — should be elaborated with more detailed data and argumentation, especially SFPs of the two languages since there has been few preceding studies accumulated on them. It will be possible to consider this as the centripetal direction.

One of the possible obstacles to this approach is that it is not the case that the only one category participates in the modal embodiment in a particular language. As shown in the table f. above, the modal system is complicated in that it consists of several independent categories: for example, auxiliaries, intonation, and tags for English.

The other direction, an extensional approach, is to expand the line developed so far in this chapter to a typological study of investigating in which system the interpersonal meaning is realized in each language. The ultimate goal may be that the accumulation of the data and argumentation be resulted in a system network.

Notes
1 English DPs are tentatively included in this category, hence its value is designated as ±.
2 The tonality indication with underlining is substituted with italics here.

References

Abe, Isamu. (1998) "Intonation in Japanese." in Hirst and Di Cristo (eds.) pp. 360–375.

Abercrombie, David. (1991) *Fifty years in phonetics*. Edinburgh: Edinburgh University Press.

Alcoba, Santiago., Julio Muril (1998) "Intonation in Spanish." in Hirst and Di Cristo (eds.) pp. 152–166.

Anderson, John M. and Colin J. Ewen. (1987) *Principles of dependency phonology*. Cambridge: Cambridge University Press.

Asher, R.E. and Eugene J.A. He (1981)*Towards a History of Phonetics*. Edinburgh: Edinburgh Press.

Asher, R.E. and J.M.Y. Simpson (1994) *The Encyclopedia of Language and Linguistics*. Oxford: Pergamon.

Bao, Zhiming. (1999)*The Structure of Tone*. New York, Oxford: Oxford University Press.

Beckman, Mary E. (1986) *Stress and Non-Stress Accent*. Dordrecht: Foris.

Beckman, Mary E. and Jan Edwar (1994) "Articulatory Evidence for Differentiating Stress Categories." in Keating (ed.)

Benkirane, Thami. (1998) "Intonation in Western Arabic (Morocco)." in Hirst and Di Cristo (eds.) pp. 345–359.

Blake, Barry. (2007) *Playing with Words: Humour in the English Language*. London: Equinox.

Bloor, Thomas. and Meriel Bloor. (2004)*The Functional Analysis of English. (second edition)* London: Arnold.

Bolinger, Dwight. (1961) *Generality, Gradience, and the All-or-None.* 's-Gravenhage: Mouton.

Bolinger, Dwight. (1978) "Intonation across languages." in Greenberg (ed.).

Bolinger, Dwight. (1986) *Intonation and Its Parts: Melody in Spoken English*. Stanford: Stanford University Press.

Bolinger, Dwight. (1989) *Intonation and Its Uses: Melody in Grammar and Discourse*. Stanford: Stanford University Press.

Bolinger, Dwight. (1998) "Intonation in American English." in Hirst and Di Cristo (eds.) pp. 45–55.

Booij, Geert. (1995) *The phonology of Dutch*. Oxford: Clarendon.

Buckley, Eugene. (1994) *Theoretical aspects of Kashaya phonology and morphology*. Stanford: CSLI.

Botinis, Antonis. (1998) "Intonation in Greek." in Hirst and Di Cristo (eds.) pp. 288–310.

Brazil, David. (1995) *A Grammar of Speech*. Oxford: Oxford University Press.

Brown, Gillian. and George Yule. (1983) *Discourse Analysis*. Cambridge: CUP.

Carr, Philip (1993) *Phonology*. Hampshire: MacMillan.

Catford, J.C. (1988) *A practical introduction to phonetics*. Oxford: Clarendon.

Chomsky, Noam. and Morris Halle. (1968) *The sound pattern of English*. New York: Harper & Row.

Colarusso, John, (1988) *The Northwest Caucasian languages*. New York: Garland.

Comrie, Bernard. (ed.) (1987) *The world's major languages*. London: Croom Helm.

Cook, Norman D. (2002) *Tone of Voice and Mind*. Amsterdam: John Benjamins.

Couper-Kuhlen, Elizabeth. (1996) *Prosody in Conversation: Interactional Studies*. Cambridge: Cambridge University Press.

Crothers, John. (1978) "Typology and universals of vowel systems." in Greenberg *et al.* (eds.).

138

Cruz-Ferreira, Madalena. (1998) "Intonation in European Portuguese." in Hirst and Di Cristo (eds.) pp. 167–178.

Cruttenden, Alan. (1997) *Intonation*. (second edition) Cambridge: Cambridge University Press.

Daneš, František. (ed.) (1974) *Papers on Functional Sentence Perspective*. Den Haag: Mouton.

Dascălu-Jinga, Laurenţia. (1998) "Intonation in Romanian." in Hirst and Di Cristo (eds.) pp. 239–260.

Dauzat, Albert. (1947) *Le Génie de la Langue Française*. Paris: Payot.

Davis, Stuart. (1988) *Topics in syllable geometry*. New York: Garland.

Dell, François. (1985) *Les règle et les sons*. Paris: Hermann.

Di Cristo, Albert. (1998) "Intonation in French." in Hirst and Di Cristo (eds.) pp. 195–218.

Đo The DIng., Tran Thien Hu'ong, and Georges Boulkia. (1998) "Intonation in Vietnamese."in Hirst & Di Cristo. (eds.)

Dressler, Wolfgang U., Hans C. Luschützky, Oskar E. Pfeiffer and John R. Rennison. (eds.) (1992) *Phonologica 1988*. Cambridge: Cambridge University Press.

Duanmu, San. (2000)*The Phonology of Standard Chinese*. Oxford: Oxford University Press.

Eggins, Suzanne. (2004)*An Introduction to Systemic Functional Linguistics. (second edition)* London: Continuum.

Esser, Jürgen. (1988) *Comparing Reading and Speaking Intonation*. Amsterdam: Rodopi.

Firth, John R. (1957) *Papers in Linguistics 1934–1951* Oxford: Oxford University Press.

Fónagy, Ivan. (1998) "Intonation in Hungarian." in Hirst and Di Cristo (eds.) pp. 328–344.

Fukuda, Kazuo. (2006) *Theme-Rheme Structure: A Functional Approach to English and Japanese*. Niigata: Niigata University.

Gårding, Eva. (1998) "Intonation in Swedish." in Hirst and Di Cristo (eds.) pp. 112–130.

Gibbon, Dafydd. (1998) "Intonation in German." in Hirst and Di Cristo (eds.) pp. 78–95.

Giegerich, Heinz J. (1992) *English phonology*. Cambridge: Cambridge University Press.

Goldsmith, John A. (ed.) (1995) *The Handbook of Phonological Theory*. Cambridge, MA: Blackwell.

Goldsmith, M. (1994) "Tone languages." in Asher et al. (eds.)

Gonzalez, Mike. et al. (1992) *Spanish dictionary*. New York: Macmillan.

Greaves, William S. (1998) *Cracking the Code: Intonation in English*. A paper presented at the Conference of Japan Association of Systemic Functional Linguistics, Oct. 1998.

Greenberg, Joseph. et al. (eds.) (1978) *Universals of human language vol. 2 Phonology*. Stanford: Stanford University Press.

Grønnum, Nina. (1998) "Intonation in Danish." in Hirst and Di Cristo (eds.) pp. 78–95.

Gussenhoven, Carlos. (1986) "The intonation of George and Mildred: post-nuclar generalizations." in John-Lewis (ed.).

Gussenhoven, Carlos. (1992) "Intonational phrasing and the prosodic hierarchy." in Dressler *et al.* (eds.).

Gussenhoven, Carlos. (2004) *The Phonology of Tone and Intonation*. Cambridge: Cambridge University Press.

Haberland, Hartmut. (1994) "Danish." in Konig, Ekkehard. and Johan van der Auwera (eds.) *The Germanic languages*. London: Routledge.

Halliday, M.A.K. (1967a) *Intonation and grammar in British English*. The Hague: Mouton.

Halliday, M.A.K. (1967b) *"Notes on Transitivity and Theme in English." (Part 1, 2, 3) Journal of Linguistics. Vols. 3, 4.*

Halliday, M.A.K. (1970) *A course in spoken English: Intonation*. London: Oxford University Press.

Halliday, M.A.K. (1973) *Explorations in the Functions of Language*. London: Edward Arnold.

Halliday, M.A.K. (1974) "The Place of 'Functional Sentence Perspective' in the System of Linguistic Description." in Daneš (ed.).

Halliday, M.A.K. (1979) "Modes of Meaning and Modes of Expressions." reprinted in Halliday (2002).

Halliday, M.A.K. (1981) "The Origin and Early Development of Chinese Phonological Theory." In R.E. Asher and Eugene J.A. Henderson. (eds.) Towards a History of Phonetics.

Halliday, M.A.K. (1985a) *An Introduction to Functional Grammar*. (first edition) London: Edward Arnold.

Halliday, M.A.K. (1985b) Spoken and Written Language. Geelong: Deakin University Press.

Halliday, M.A.K. (1994) *An Introduction to Functional Grammar*. (second edition) London: Edward Arnold.

Halliday, M.A.K. (2002) *On Grammar*. London: Continuum.

Halliday, M.A.K. and Christian Matthiessen. (2004) *An Introduction to Functional Grammar*. (third edition) London: Arnold.

Halliday, M.A.K. and Christian Matthiessen. (2014) *Halliday's Introduction to Functional Grammar*. (fourth edition) London: Routledge.

Halliday, M.A.K. and William S Greaves. (2008) *Intonation in the Grammar of English*. London: Equinox.

Halliday, M.A.K. (1996) "On grammar and grammatics." in Hasan *et al.* (eds.)

Halliday, M.A.K. and Ruqaiya Hasan. (1976) *Cohesion in English*. Harlow: Longman.

Hasan, Ruqaiya., Carmel Cloran, David Butt. (eds.) (1996) *Functional descriptions: theory in practice*. Amsterdam: John Benjamins.

Harris, John. (1994) *English sound structure*. Oxford: Basil Blackwell.

Harris, J.W. (1983) *Syllable Structure and Stress in Spanish: A Non Linear Analysis*. Cambridge, MA.: MIT Press.

Hinds, John., Senko K. Meynard and Shoichi Iwasaki. (eds.) (1987) *Perspectives on topicalization: the case of Japanese 'wa'*. Amsterdam: John Benjamins.

Hirst, Daniel. (1998) "Intonation in British English." in Hirst and Di Cristo (eds.) pp. 56–77.

Hirst, Daniel. and Albert Di Cristo. (1998a) "A survey of intonation systems."in Hirst and Di Cristo (eds.)

Hirst, Daniel. and Albert Di Cristo. (eds.) (1998b) *Intonation systems: a survey of twenty languages*. Cambridge: Cambridge University Press.

Hockett, Charles F. (1958) *A course in modern linguistics*. New York: MacMillan.

Holes, Clive. (1995) *Modern Arabic*. London: Longman.

Hulst, Harry van der. and Norval Smith. (eds.) (1982) *The structure of phonological representation* (Part II). Dordrecht: Foris.

Iivonen, Antti. (1998) "Intonation in Finnish." in Hirst and Di Cristo (eds.) pp. 313–327.

Itô, Junko. (1990) "Prosodic minimality in Japanese." in Ziolkowski et al. (eds.).

Johns-Lewis, Catherine. (ed.) (1986) *Intonation in Discourse*. London: Croom Helm.

Johnson, Keith. (1997) *Acoustic and auditory phonetics*. Cambridge, MA.: Blackwell.

Jones, Daniel. (1950a) *An outline of English phonetics (Seventh edition)*. Cambridge: W. Heffer & Sons.

Jones, Daniel. (1950b) *The phoneme: its nature and use*. Cambridge: W. Heffer & Sons.

Jones, Daniel. (1956) *The pronunciation of English* (fourth edition). Cambridge: W. Heffer & Sons.

Kadooka, Ken-ichi (1990) *A Contrastive Study of the Vowel Systems of English, Japanese and Mandarin Chinese*. Unpublished Master's Thesis submitted to Kobe University.

Kadooka, Ken-Ichi. (1996a) "Typology on the vowel systems." *Ryukoku Studies in English Language and Literature* vol. 15. pp. 84–103.

Kadooka, Ken-Ichi. (1996b) "Some aspects around the notion *syllable*." *The Ryukoku Journal of Humanities and Sciences* Vol. 18 no. 1. pp. 35–51.

Kadooka, Ken-Ichi. (1997) "CV Variations and Relative Productivity."in *The Ryukoku Journal of Humanities and Sciences*. Vol. 23. No. 1.

Kadooka, Ken-Ichi. (1998a) "A Cross-linguistic Survey of Syllable Inventories: Methodology and Procedure." in *Hyogo University Journal*. Vol. 3. pp. 85–99.

Kadooka, Ken-Ichi. (1998b) "Orthography and phonology."『貝田守教授停年退官記念論文集』大阪外国語大学.

Kadooka, Ken-Ichi. (1999a) "Phonetic and/or phonological symmetry of the vowel systems." in *Phonological Studies* Vol. 2. The Phonological Society of Japan.

Kadooka, KenIchi. (1999b) "English intonation system as interpersonal embodiment: contrast with Japanese and Chinese particles." *Ryukoku Studies in English Language and Literature* vol. 18.

Kadooka, KenIchi. (1999c) "Defining the symmetry of vowel systems." *Kobe Papers in Linguistics*. vol. 2. Kobe: Kobe University.

Kadooka, Ken-Ichi. (2000) "A Contrastive Study of Function in Intonation Systems (part 1)." in *Ryukoku Studies in English Language and Literature*. vol. 19.

Kadooka, Ken-Ichi. (2001a) "A contrastive study on the realization of interpersonal nuances." in *The Ryukoku Journal of Humanities and Sciences*. Vol. 23. No. 1.

Kadooka, Ken-Ichi. (2001b) "A Note on the Interpersonal-Nuance Carriers in Japanese." in *JASFL Occasional Papers*. Vol. 2. pp. 17–28.

Kadooka, Ken-Ichi. (2002) "How intonation works in tone languages?" in *The Ryukoku Journal of Humanities and Sciences*. Vol. 23. No. 2.

Kadooka, Ken-Ichi. (2003) "A Systemic Analysis of Intonation System of English." in *The Ryukoku Journal of Humanities and Sciences*. vol. 24. No. 2. pp. 13–27.

Kadooka, Ken-Ichi. (2004a) "On the Multi-Layer Structure of Metafunctions." in *JASFL Occasional Papers*. Vol. 3. pp. 43–62.

Kadooka, Ken-Ichi. (2004b) "A Systemic Approach to the Typology of Functions in Intonation Systems." in *Festschrift for Professor Masayoshi Shibatani's Sixtieth Birthday*. Edited by Taro Kageyama and Hideki Kishimoto. Tokyo: Kurosio. pp. 389–404.

Kadooka, Ken-Ichi. (2006) "A Systemic Account on Strata and the Meaning of Intonation." in *The Ryukoku Journal of Humanities and Sciences*. vol. 27. No. 2. pp. 43–58.

Kadooka, Ken-Ichi. (2009) "Punch Line Paratone: A Special Use of Discourse Intonation." *The Ryukoku Journal of Humanities and Sciences* Vol. 31, No. 1. pp. 203–220.

Kadooka, Ken-Ichi. (2011a) "Rakugo no Danwa-teki Kouzou (The Discourse Structure of the Rakugo Stories)." *Ryukoku International Center Research Bulletin*. Vol. 20.

Kadooka, Ken-Ichi. (2011b) "An Acoustic Analysis of the Punch Line Paratone in English Jokes." *The Ryukoku Journal of Humanities and Sciences* Vol. 33, No. 1. pp. 1–13.

Kadooka, Ken-Ichi. (2012a) "An Acoustic Analysis of the Punch Line Paratone in the Japanese *Kobanashi Stories*." *The Ryukoku Journal of Humanities and Sciences* Vol. 33, No. 2. pp. 17–37.

Kadooka, Ken-Ichi. (2013) "An Acoustic Analysis English Monologue- and Dialogue-type Jokes." *The Ryukoku Journal of Humanities and Sciences* Vol. 34, No. 2. pp. 21–36.

Kadooka, Ken-ichi. (2018) *A Linguistic Study of Kamigata Rakugo*. Tokyo: Shohakusha.

Karlgren, Bernhard. (1949) *The Chinese Language*. New York: Ronal Press. Translation into Japanese by: Nobukazu Ohara, Tetsuo Tsujii, Takashi Aiura, and Tatsuo Nishida. Tokyo: Konan Shoin, 1958.

Kaufman, Terrence. (1994) "The Native Languages of Meso-America." in Moseley and Asher (eds.).

Keating, Patricia A. (ed.) (1994) *Phonological Structure and Phonetic Form: Papers in Laboratory Phonology III*. Cambridge: Cambridge University Press.

Kraft, Charles H. & A.H.M. Kir (1973) *Hausa*. London: Hodder & Stoughton.

Kratochvil, Paul. (1998) "Intonation in Beijing Chinese." in Hirst and Di Cristo. (eds., 1998).

Kreidler, Charles W. (1989)*The Pronunciation of English*. New York: Basil Blackwell.

Ladd, D. Robert., Klaus Schere (1986) "An integrated approach to studying intonation and attitude." in John-Lewis (ed.).

Ladd, D. Robert. (1996) *Intonational Phonology*. Cambridge: Cambridge University Press.

Ladefoged, Peter. (1982) *A course in phonetics* (second edition). New York: Harcourt Brace Jovanovich.

Ladefoged, Peter. and Ian Maddieson. (1996) *The sounds of the world's languages*. Oxford: Basil Blackwell.

Lass, Roger. (1984) *Phonology*. Cambridge: Cambridge University Press.

Laver, John. (1994) *Principles of phonetics*. Cambridge: Cambridge University Press.

Lewis, Edwin C. (1992) *Welsh dictionary*. London: Hodder and Stoughton.

Lindau, Mona. (1975) *Features for vowels*. Los Angeles: UCLA.

Luksaneeyanawin, Sudaporn. (1998) "Intonation in Thai." in Hirst and di Cristo. (eds., 1998).

McCawley, James D. (1968) *The phonological component of a grammar of Japanese*. The Hague: Mouton.

Maddieson, Ian. (1984) *Patterns of sounds*. Cambridge: Cambridge University Press.

Magazis, George A. (1990) *Standard Greek dictionary*. Berlin: Langenscheidt

Matthews, Stephen. and Virginia Yip. (1994) *Cantonese*. London: Routledge.

Misheva, Anastasia. And Michel Nikov. (1998) "Intonation in Bulgarian." in Hirst and Di Cristo (eds.) pp. 275–287.

Moraes, de Aoão Antônio. (1998) "Intonation in Brazilian Portuguese." in Hirst and Di Cristo (eds.) pp. 179–194.

Moseley, Christopher. and R.E. (1994)*Atlas of the World's Languages*. New York: Routledge.

O'Connor, J. D. and G.F. Arnold (1973) *Intonation of colloquial English* (second edition). Japanese translation by Katayama *et al.* (1994) Tokyo: Nan'un-do.

Odden, David. (1995) "Tone: African Languages." in Goldsmith (ed.).

Okazaki, Masao. (1998) *English Sentence Prosody: The Interface between Sound and Meaning*. Tokyo: Kaitakusha.

Osada, Toshiki. (1992) *A reference grammar of Mundari*. Tokyo: Institute for the Study of Languages and Cultures of Asia and Africa.

Pennington, Martha C. (ed.) (2007) *Phonology in Context*. Hampshire: Palgrave.

Peyrollaz, Marguerite., M.-L. (1954) *Manuel de Phonéteique et de Diction Françaises*. Paris: Larousse.

Pheby, John. (1975) *Intonation und Grammatik im Deutschen*. Berlin: Akademie Verlag.

Pierrehumbert, Janet B., and Mary E. Beckman. (1988) *Japanese tone structure*. Cambridge, MA.: The MIT Press.

Pike, Kenneth L. (1945) *The Intonation of American English*. Westport, Conn.: Greenwood Press.

Pierrehumbert, Janet B., and Mary E. Beckman. (1988) *Japanese tone structure*. Cambridge, MA.: The MIT Press.

Pontifex, Zsuzsa. (1993) *Hungarian*. London: Hodder and Stoughton.

Quirk, Randolph., Sidney Greenbaum, Geoffrey Leech, Jan Svartvik. (1985) *A comprehensive grammar of the English language.* London: Longman.

Renier, Fernand G. (1981) *Colloquial Dutch* (Third edition). London: Routledge.

Rossi, Mario. (1998) "Intonation in Italian." in Hirst and Di Cristo (eds.) pp. 219–238.

Schourup, Lawrence C. (1985) *Common discourse particles in English conversation.* New York: Garland.

Shang, Yongqing., Tooru Hishinuma. *et al.* (1992) *Zhong-Ri Cidian* (中日辞典). Tokyo: Shogakukan.

Shibatani, Masayoshi. (1990) *The Languages of Japan.* Cambridge: Cambridge University Press.

Smyth, David. (1995) *Thai.* London: Hodder & Stoughton.

Sofroniou, S.A. (1962) *Modern Greek.* Lodon: Hodder and Stoughton.

Suzuki, Shintaro. et al. (1987) *Nouveau dictionaire standard français-japonais.* Tokyo: Taishukan.

Svetozarova, Natalia. (1998) "Intonation in Russian." in Hirst and Di Cristo (eds.) pp. 261–274.

Sweet, Henry. (1888) *A History of English Sounds: From the Earliest Period.* Oxford: Clarendon Press.

Sweet, Henry. (1900) *A English Grammar: Logical and Historical. (Part 1)* Oxford: Clarendon Press.

Sweet, Henry. (1906) *A Primer of Phonetics. (Third edition, revised)* Oxford: Clarendon Press.

Tench, Paul. (1992) "From Prosodic Analysis to Systemic Phonology." in Tench (ed.).

Tench, Paul. (ed.) (1992) *Studies in Systemic Phonology.* London: Pinter.

Tench, Paul. (1996) *The intonation system of English.* London: Cassell.

't Hart, Johan. (1998) "Intonation in Dutch." in Hirst and Di Cristo (eds.) pp. 112–130.

Trnka, Bohumil. (1968) *A phonological analysis of present-day standard English.* (New revised and updated edition). Alabama: University of Alabama Press.

Trubetzkoy, N.S. (1939) *Grundzüge der Phonologie.* Traduction française par J. Cantineau. Paris: Klinsieck, 1967.

Trager, George L. and Henry Le (1957)*An Outline of English Structure.* Washington, D.C.: American Council of LearnedSocieties.

Trnka, Bohumil. (1968) *A Phonological Analysis of Present-day Standard English.* Alabama: University of Alabama Press.

Vance, Timothy. (1987) *An introduction to Japanese phonology.* Albany, NY: State University of New York Press.

van der Hulst, Harry. and Keit (1993)*The phonology of tone.* Berlin: Mouton de Gruyter.

Watt, David L. E. (1992) "An instrumental analysis of English nuclear tones." in Tench (ed.).

Wennerstrom, Ann. (2001) *The Music of Everyday Speech.* Oxford University Press, Oxford.

Wichmann, Anne. (2000) *Intonation in Text and Discourse: Beginnings, middles and ends.* Harlow: Pearson Education.

Wiese, Richard. (1996) *The Phonology of German.* Oxford: Clarendon.

Yip, Moira. (1995) "Tone in East Asian Languages." in Goldsmith (ed.).

Yip, Moira. (2002) *Tone.* Cambridge: Cambridge University Press.

Young, David. (1992) "English consonant clusters: a systemic approach." in Tench (ed.) *Studies in systemic phonology.* London: Pinter.

Ziolkowski, Michael., Manuela Noske, Karen Deaton. (eds.) (1990) *Papers from the 26th Regional Meeting of the Chicago Linguistic Society. Volume 2.* Chicago: Chicago Linguistic Society.

REFERENCES

ブロック、バーナード、ジョー（1980）『言語分析の概要』玉崎孫治訳。南雲堂（原著：*Outline of Linguistc Analysis*. By Bernard Bloch and George L. Trager.）

キャンベル、ニック（1997）『プラグマティック・イントネーション：韻律情報の機能的役割』音声文法研究会（編）pp. 55–74.

キャンベル、ニック（1999）「韻律解釈における基本単位」音声文法研究会（編）

橋本萬太郎（1989）「中国語」『言語学大辞典』第2巻、三省堂

早田輝洋（1999）『音調のタイポロジー』大修館書店

稗田乃（1992）「ルオ語」『言語学大辞典』第4巻、三省堂

角岡賢一（2006）「ことばをあやつる　音調と意味の関係」龍城（編）所収

角岡賢一（2009）『節音調の機能についての選択体系文法による分析』成美堂

片桐恭弘（1997）『終助詞とイントネーション』音声文法研究会（編）

城生佰太郎（1998）『日本語音声科学』バンダイミュージックエンタテインメント

窪薗晴夫（1995）『語形成と音韻構造』くろしお出版

神尾昭雄（1990）『情報のなわ張り理論　言語の機能的分析』大修館書店

神尾昭雄（2002）『続・情報のなわ張り理論』大修館書店

亀井孝、河野六郎、千野栄一編（1989）『言語学大辞典』第2巻、三省堂

金田一春彦（1991）『日本語音韻の研究』（第10版）東京堂出版

金田一春彦（2001）『日本語音韻音調史の研究』吉川弘文館

金田一春彦（2004）『金田一春彦著作集　第四巻』玉川大学出版部

金田一京助（編）（1997）『新明解国語事典』（第5版）三省堂

小谷晋一郎（2002）『英語の談話文法』同朋社

郡史郎（1997）「日本語のイントネーション―型と機能―」杉藤・国広（編）所収

河野守夫（2001）『音声言語の認識と生成のメカニズム：ことばの時間制御機構とその役割』金星堂

香坂順一（1974）『中国語学の基礎知識』（訂正版）光生館

香坂順一（1989）『中国語軽声辞典』光生館

窪薗晴夫（1999）『日本語の音声』岩波書店

窪薗晴夫、太田聡（1998）『音韻構造とアクセント』研究社

李思敬（1995）『音韻のはなし――中国音韻学の基礎知識』（訂正版）光生館

李敦柱（2004）『漢字音韻学の理解』藤井茂利訳。風間書房

牧村史陽（1984）『大阪ことば事典』講談社

三宅英文（2006）『選択体系機能文法と言語芸術』安田女子大学言語文化研究所

溝上富夫（1992）「パンジャーブ語」『言語学大辞典』第3巻、三省堂

オコナー、J.D.、G.F.アーノルド（1973）『イギリス英語のイントネーション』片山嘉雄、他訳。南雲堂（原著：*Intonation of colloquial English* (second edition). London: Longman.）

音声文法研究会（編）（1997）『文法と音声』くろしお出版

音声文法研究会（編）（1999）『文法と音声II』くろしお出版

音声文法研究会（編）（2001）『文法と音声III』くろしお出版

音声文法研究会（編）（2004）『文法と音声IV』くろしお出版

音声文法研究会（編）（2006）『文法と音声V』くろしお出版

大原信一（1991）『中国語と英語』（新訂版）光生堂

才田いずみ（1997）「拍・アクセントの習得支援システム」杉藤・国広（編）所収

三省堂（1988–1992）『言語学大辞典』世界言語編、三省堂

杉藤美代子（1997）「話し言葉のアクセント、イントネーション、リズムとポーズ」杉藤・国広（編）所収

杉藤美代子（1997）『音声波形は語る』和泉書院

杉藤美代子（監修）、国広哲弥、他（編）（1997）『アクセント・イントネーション・リズムとポーズ』三省堂

定延利之、中川正之（編）（2007）『音声文法の対照』くろしお出版

尚永清（編）（1992）『中日辞典』（初版）小学館

佐藤亮一、真田信治、加藤正信（1997）『諸方言のアクセントとイントネーション』三省堂

佐藤寧、佐藤努（1998）『現代の英語音声学』金星堂

清水紀佳（1988）「アフリカの諸言語」『言語学大辞典』三省堂

戴浩一、莭鳳生（編）（1994）『功能主義与漢語語法』北京：北京語言学院出版社

城田俊（1993）『日本語の音—音声学と音韻論』ひつじ書房

染田利信（1987）『音韻論の諸問題』人文書院

竹林滋（1996）『英語音声学』研究社

龍城正明（編）（2006a）『ことばは生きている』くろしお出版

龍城正明（2006b）「第3章　ことばを理解する　単語と節の関係」『ことばは生きている』くろしお出版

龍城正明（2006c）「第5章　ことばを伝える　テーマの展開」『ことばは生きている』くろしお出版

龍城正明（2008）「「は」と「が」そのメタ機能からの再考」『日本機能言語学会プロシーディングス』第2号　pp. 135–149.

時枝誠記（1978）『日本文法　口語編』岩波書店

冨田健次（1988）「ヴェトナム語」『言語学大辞典』第1巻、三省堂

藤堂明保（1957）『中国語音韻論』江南書院

角田太作（1991）『世界の言語と日本語』くろしお出版

梅田博之（1989）「朝鮮語」『言語学大辞典』第3巻、三省堂

渡辺和幸（1994）『英語イントネーション論』研究社

渡部眞一郎（1996）「母音体系の類型論」『音韻研究』音韻論研究会（編）、開拓社

楊剣橋（1996）『漢語現代音韻学』上海：复旦大学出版社

八杉佳穂（1988）「オトマンゲ語族」『言語学大辞典』第1巻、三省堂

山口登、筧壽雄（2001）『機能文法概説』くろしお出版

山本文明（1989a）「スウェーデン語」『言語学大辞典』第2巻、三省堂

山本文明（1989b）「デンマーク語」『言語学大辞典』第2巻、三省堂

Index

A
accidental gaps   121
American Structurism   38

B
baseline   57, 99, 105, 107

C
complex   37
consonant clusters   4, 119
context of situation   43
CV patterns   124
CV variations   119, 129

D
discourse particle   8, 60
discourse semantics   76
Duration   63, 92, 98, 104

E
experiential   35, 46

F
field   43, 52
final particles   21, 80
functional categories   135

G
glide   120
gradual lowering   70, 94, 108

H
High Paratone   108

I
ideational   35, 55
interpersonal   35, 44, 55, 62, 84

interpersonal metafunction   1, 13, 46, 63
interpersonal nuances   2, 21, 32, 75, 80
intonation   17, 78
intonation system   38, 50, 78
intonation units   71

K
key   77

L
lexicogrammar   43, 76, 87
logical   35, 46
Low Paratone   57

M
macro-function   42
metafunction   35, 42, 44, 56, 88
modal auxiliaries   83, 134
Modality   52, 77
mode   43
mood   47, 49, 52, 77, 88

N
New information   49

P
paratone   48, 73, 107
pitch contour   9, 58, 93
Putonghua   111
punch line   64, 67, 69, 93, 97, 103
Punch Line Paratone   57, 89
phrase final particles   76, 80, 88
PIS   18, 22
polarity   60
Pragmatic meaning   3
pragmatic intonation   18
Process type   51

prominence   20, 67, 79

prosody   4, 21

Q

qingsheng   111

R

rank   47, 75

rank scale   75

register   36

relative productivity   120

residue   47, 49, 88

rheme   47, 49, 83

RP   129, 131

S

secondary tone   59

semiotic system   76

sentence-final particle   2

SFL   1, 40, 59, 75, 88

SFPs   2, 60, 75, 85, 111, 135

SISs   22, 80

situation   43

strata   40, 47

structural gaps   120

System   36

syllable inventory   131

syllable structure   119

Systemic Functional Linguistics   1, 35

T

taxis   47

tag question   8, 60

tenor   43

textual   35, 45

theme   47, 49, 83, 88

tonality   1, 6

tone   6, 61, 77

tone concord   48

tone languages   4, 18, 32

tone sequence   48

tonic   66

tonic prominence   77

tonicity   6

V

voices   44

角岡賢一（かどおか けんいち）

略歴

神戸大学文学部文学研究科（修士課程）修
了。神戸大学大学院文化学研究科（博士課
程）単位取得。
龍谷大学経営学部講師に着任、助教授を経
て教授。

Ken-ichi Kadooka was born in 1959, BA at
Osaka University of Foreign Studies, MA
at Kobe University, PhD candidate.
Senior Lecturer, Associate Professor and
Professor at the Faculty of Business
Administration, Ryukoku University.

主な著書・論文

・『日本語オノマトペ語彙における形態
的・音韻的体系性について』（くろしお出
版、2007）
・『節音調の機能についての選択体系によ
る分析』（成美堂、2009）
・『機能文法による日本語モダリティ研究』
（編著、くろしお出版、2016）
・ *A Linguistic Study of Kamigata Rakugo*
（松柏社、2018）
・ *Japanese mood and modality in systemic
functional linguistics : theory and
application* （編著、 John Benjamins、
2021）
・『上方落語にみられる待遇表現』（くろし
お出版、2021）

そのほか紀要等論文百本超。

龍谷大学国際社会文化研究所叢書　第35巻
Hituzi Linguistics in English No.39

A Contrastive Study of
Function in Intonation Systems

発行	2024年11月5日 初版1刷
定価	8000円＋税
著者	◎角岡賢一
発行者	松本功
ブックデザイン	白井敬尚形成事務所
印刷・製本所	亜細亜印刷株式会社
発行所	株式会社 ひつじ書房

〒112-0011　東京都文京区
千石2-1-2　大和ビル2F
Tel: 03-5319-4916
Fax: 03-5319-4917
郵便振替00120-8-142852
toiawase@hituzi.co.jp
https://www.hituzi.co.jp/
ISBN978-4-8234-1257-8

造本には充分注意しておりますが、
落丁・乱丁などがございましたら、
小社かお買上げ書店にて
おとりかえいたします。
ご意見、ご感想など、小社まで
お寄せ下されば幸いです。

Hituzi Linguistics in English

No. 35　English Prepositions in Usage Contexts
A Proposal for a Construction-Based Semantics
堀内ふみ野 著　定価 9,400 円 + 税

No. 36　Integrated Skills Development
Comprehending and Producing Texts in a Foreign Language
中森誉之 著　定価 11,000 円 + 税

No. 37　Perception and Linguistic Form
A Cognitive Linguistic Analysis of the Copulative Perception Verb
Construction
徳山聖美 著　定価 11,000 円 + 税

No. 38　The *No More A than B* Construction
A Cognitive and Pragmatic Approach
廣田篤 著　定価 12,000 円 + 税